GOOD AND PROPER
MATERIALS

This oil-painting by G. Forster shows the typical brickmaking processes in mid nineteenth-century London. It depicts William Nash's brickfield at Edmonton in 1856, situated south of the present Church Street

Reproduced from the original in the possession of London Brick Company

(Photograph by the Royal Commission on the Historical Monuments of England)

GOOD AND PROPER
MATERIALS

THE FABRIC OF LONDON
SINCE THE GREAT FIRE

Papers given at a conference
organised by the Survey of London
at the Society of Antiquaries
on 21 October 1988

Edited by
HERMIONE HOBHOUSE
and
ANN SAUNDERS

The Royal Commission
on the Historical
Monuments of England
in association with
The London Topographical Society
Publication No. 140

1989

© London Topographical Society

Publication no. 140 of the
London Topographical Society
3 Meadway Gate, London NW11

ISBN 0 902 087 27 4

General Editor: Ann Loreille Saunders PhD, FSA

PRINTED IN GREAT BRITAIN BY
W. S. MANEY & SON LTD, HUDSON ROAD, LEEDS

CONTENTS

FOREWORD

Somebody once wrote of London as the 'unknown city'. This conveys some truth — there is much more to be learned and understood about how London has developed into the city that it now is; but it is a misleading label if it suggests that any city is fully known, or indeed knowable. A modern metropolis is compounded of so many elements derived from so many kinds of influence — geographical, social, demographic, economic, political — that one may despair of ever understanding it fully. But one may hope to join in bringing together fragments of evidence which will slowly accumulate to help in building up a reasonably convincing interpretation of what we know. Each generation should have something to contribute.

One element in the structure of London has been curiously little studied in detail: the materials used in its buildings. This was the subject of a day-long seminar meeting organised by the Survey of London branch of the Royal Commission on the Historical Monuments of England and held in the Society of Antiquaries' rooms in Burlington House on 21 October 1988. The six papers presented then are now printed. Between them they offer introductions — no more — to the study of brick, timber, stucco, terracotta, iron, and mechanical services in London buildings. Stone does not appear because it has been fairly fully studied, though it cannot be taken for granted that we know all we want to know about it; concrete construction must wait for another day; and roofing materials still need examination.

What is here is as much as could be imbibed in a single day, and it seems valuable to put it out to a wider readership, to encourage development of inquiry and publication on this fundamental subject. I hope that these essays will be enjoyed for themselves and will stimulate more research. They show that the subject is not only important in an academic sense but can also be entertaining. It is not about high art but about the structural envelope of everyday life. Knowledge of it illuminates much that is so commonplace as to be obscure. Yet, as Conan Doyle observed in a different connection, 'depend upon it, there is nothing so unnatural as the commonplace'.

MICHAEL ROBBINS

NOTES ON CONTRIBUTORS

CHARLES BROOKING Curator of the Brooking Collection Trust, Woodhay, White Lane, Guildford, Surrey GU4 8PU. Architectural Historian, Collector, and expert on architectural fittings and furnishings.

ALAN COX Assistant Editor, *Survey of London*, Newlands House, 37–40 Berners St, London W1P 4BP. Formerly assistant Conservation Officer with Bedfordshire County Council, with responsibility for the County Sites and Monuments Record.
Author of *Brickmaking: A History and Gazetteer*, the first volume in the *Survey of Bedfordshire* (jointly published by Bedfordshire County Council and RCHME).

IAN GRANT FRIBA, 41 Ladbroke Square, London W11. Architect in private practice, has worked at the Wallace Collection, Reform Club and the Palace of Westminster. Founder Member of the Victorian Society, expert on interior decoration of the nineteenth century.

HERMIONE HOBHOUSE MBE, FSA, General Editor, *Survey of London*, Newlands House, 37–40 Berners Street, London W1P 4BP. Urban historian and conservationist, former Secretary Victorian Society, author of works on nineteenth-century London, including *Thomas Cubitt: Master Builder*, and *Lost London*.

FRANK KELSALL Inspector of Historic Buildings, English Heritage, Room 335, Fortress House, 23 Savile Row, London W1X 2HE: with responsibility for the east Midlands and north-west of England.
Treasurer, and formerly Secretary, of the Society of Architectural Historians of Great Britain. Has written much on London buildings, and, of particular interest to this conference, published an account of Liardet Stucco in *Architectural History*, 27.

MICHAEL ROBBINS CBE, President of the Society of Antiquaries, Chairman of the Board of Governors of the Museum of London. Author of *Middlesex* (1953) and, with T. C. Barker, *History of London Transport* (2 vols, 1963 and 1974).

ANN SAUNDERS Ph.D., FSA, Hon. Editor, London Topographical Society, writer and lecturer. Books include *Regent's Park* (1969, 1981) and *The Art and Architecture of London* (1984, 1987).

MICHAEL STRATTON Ph.D. Ironbridge Institute, The Ironbridge Gorge Museum, Ironbridge, Telford, Shropshire TF8 7AW. Lecturer in Industrial Archaeology in the Department of Economic and Social History at the University of Birmingham. Also a qualified Town Planner, and leading authority on the manufacture and use of architectural ceramics. Author of several architectural studies.

JAMES SUTHERLAND F.Eng., FICE, consultant (previously partner) Harris & Sutherland, civil and structural engineers. Currently President of the Newcomen Society for the Study of the History of Science and Technology, Convenor of Institution of Structural Engineers History Group and a member of the Royal Fine Art Commission. Has lectured and written quite widely on the history of engineering.

DAVID YEOMANS Ph.D. Lecturer in the Department of Architecture and Building Engineering, University of Liverpool, Leverhulme Building, Abercromby Square, P.O. Box 147, Liverpool L69 3BX. Formerly Chief Education Officer at the Timber Research and Development Association, and member of the ICOMOS UK Wood Committee. Has written mostly on the history of timber roof structures.

INTRODUCTION

by HERMIONE HOBHOUSE

After the Great Fire, London was rebuilt as a city of brick and stone, and this is still true today, though a wide variety of other materials have been developed since. This conference was planned to give London historians an opportunity to look at the fabric of the city through the materials of which it is constructed. Though other types of buildings were discussed, the emphasis was on traditional London buildings of the terrace house format, that with brick bearing walls with timber joists and beams, with later developments into stucco and terracotta, and with iron replacing timber for some uses.

There were several good reasons for choosing this theme. First of all, the materials most abundant locally or permitted by local authorities for reasons of health or fire prevention have a great effect on town planning and architecture, which makes the post-Fire rebuilding a watershed. Looking at buildings from the point of view of what they were built of, rather than primarily how they are designed gives a valuable change of perspective.

Secondly, of course, there is the interest of the materials themselves. Though the ready availability of 'argillaceous clay', to use John Britton's phrase, made London a brick city, often constructed out of brickearth dug from the spot on which the houses were erected, brick is of course a most versatile material, susceptible of a wide variety of colours and shapes. As transport improved and became cheaper, then an even wider palette of bricks and terracotta was available to the architect and designer.

Thirdly, there is still not enough information available on the dating of London materials, though, as these talks demonstrate, scholars are beginning to address the problems of where materials came from, and when they were most common, as well as the more traditional question of why they were fashionable among both architects and the public.

Finally, the conference was promoted in the hope that it would stimulate an interest in using some of the techniques developed for archaeological exploration on buildings of more modern times. Relatively little information is available to date bricks or timber from the eighteenth and nineteenth centuries with any precision. More emphasis on materials would make it possible to have an objective way of dating buildings to set against the traditional subjective approach, through design, of the architectural historian.

Historians working in post-Fire London have a large range of written sources, pattern books, encyclopaedias, and the professional press, to enable them to date materials as well as styles. The collection of building materials made by Charles Brooking provides a valuable opportunity for both dating original construction, and identifying later alterations, both internal and external, like refenestration. Extension of these techniques, and greater use of them to collate written and archaeological evidence, would make much more information available to the historian of 'modern' London.

These papers are very much a beginning, both to what it is hoped may become an occasional series of conferences organised on London topics by the *Survey of London*, and to the subject. None the less they provide a wide and substantial introduction, with the London brick, made from its native clay, the 'improvements' in stucco and plaster and later the adornments of terracotta. Structural timber and iron are very large subjects, but their development is sketched out in two expert papers. Finally, comes George Augustus Sala's modern London house, the 'house that is

. . . solidly furnished from top to toe, with every modern convenience and improvement: . . . with patent grates, patent door-handles, dish-lifts, asbestos stoves, gas cooking ranges, and excruciatingly complicated ventilating contrivances'. These are dealt with by an archaeologically minded collector, and a practising architect, working to restore the patent door-handles, if not 'the excruciatingly complicated' ventilators.

The most important material absent from this book is stone in its many forms so familiar to Londoners — monumental Portland, and its cheaper cousin Bath, ragstone for Gothic churches, Yorkshire stone for pavements, 'square Jersey pebble' for thoroughfares, slate from Wales and Westmorland for roofs, even the occasional piece of marble. The reason was, of course, the problem of time, since it was clear that the subject would need a whole day to do it justice. However, it is to be hoped that this collection of papers may stimulate demand, and make a further conference on London materials possible in the future.

BRICKS TO BUILD A CAPITAL

by ALAN COX

'The Earth about *London*, rightly managed, will yield as good Brick as were the *Roman* bricks . . . and will endure, in our Air, beyond any Stone our Island affords'.[1] The words are those of Christopher Wren, who as Surveyor of the Office of Works, ushered in with such finely executed brick buildings as The Orangery at Kensington, the Royal Hospital at Chelsea, and the Wren Building at Hampton Court, what is commonly regarded as the Golden Age of English brickwork. Wren was also of course a Commissioner for the Rebuilding of London after the Great Fire, and London after 1666 became predominantly a brick-built city. This was due in part to the stipulations (which had begun before the Fire but had been inadequately enforced) that rebuilding should be in brick or stone. Both were fire-resistant, but brick was cheaper, was more readily available in the London area, was on the whole easier to work with, was regarded as being more durable than most stones, and most importantly was becoming increasingly fashionable. Indeed developments of the 1630s and 1640s like Covent Garden and the south side of Great Queen Street (unfortunately neither of which has survived) were already being built of brick before the Fire[2] and there is little doubt that London would have become a brick city even without the impetus of the disaster.

The result is a rich and varied heritage of brick buildings, in which we should not overlook the Victorian period, which has many claims to be a second Golden Age of brickwork, nor even our own century with, for example, the fine brickwork employed by Sir Giles Gilbert Scott. It is also as well to remind ourselves that much of this brick inheritance is hidden, not only behind stucco and plaster but also within many seemingly stone edifices such as the Foreign Office, the Houses of Parliament, Tower Bridge, or the Law Courts. The last of these, while presenting a public face of stone to the Strand, is assertively brick along much of the side and rear elevations to Bell Yard and Carey Street. In fact some thirty-five million bricks were used in the construction of the building.[3]

In this paper just two aspects of London's brick heritage will be considered: how the bricks were made and to a lesser extent where they were made.

First the traditional methods of hand-brickmaking, particularly of London stock bricks, will be examined, indicating where London practices differed from the rest of the country. It should, however, be pointed out that the term 'stock brick' originally meant a brick made on a stock (this latter term will be explained when the process of moulding is described below). In the seventeenth and eighteenth centuries 'stock' was applied to good facing bricks as opposed to 'place' bricks, which were cheap, underburnt bricks, only suitable for common brickwork, that is for work not intended to be left exposed.[4] Used in general terms, therefore, stock brick is not a very meaningful description, but the London stock brick was a clearly recognised and recognisably distinct type of brick.

The manufacture of London stocks seems to have begun almost immediately after the Great Fire, in the 1670s,[5] and the methods of manufacture varied little over the next two, or two and a half centuries. The stock brick is made from the London Clay, a superficial deposit of brickearth which is naturally the easiest clay from which to make bricks, that is without the benefit of any mechanical refinements. This brickearth generally, and fortunately for London, occurs along river valleys,[6] and it seems that almost from the outset some London stocks were brought up the

Thames from Kent to the City.[7] In its pure state it was referred to as 'malm', and 'malms' or malm bricks were considered the best type of London stock brick.[8] The brickearth is high in silica (about sixty-five to seventy-five per cent), low in alumina (eight to eleven per cent), and with a higher than usual lime content of between seven and nine per cent.[9] Normally the iron oxide in a clay will tend to produce red brick but lime will nullify this and produce a characteristic yellow- or white-coloured brick (this is true of any yellowish or whitish brick whether it be a London stock, a Suffolk white, or a yellow gault). The lime also diminishes the amount of contraction during the drying of the raw bricks and in addition acts as a flux combining with the silica of the clay to produce a durable, generally well-burnt brick.[10] The colour of stocks could, in fact, vary quite considerably from a deep earthy purplish colour to a bright yellow, but somewhat confusingly they were generally referred to as 'greys' or 'grey stocks'.

The discovery of new sources of clay for stocks was always done on the best scientific lines: a group of men would gather in a likely field and the experienced brickmakers would pop a piece of clay in their mouths; by the taste and feel they could tell whether the clay was suitable or not.[11]

The clay was dug by hand using pick and shovel, though a peculiar digging tool evolved for the purpose, like a cross between a spade and a fork — it had three prongs with a bar or blade across the bottom.[12] Clay was best dug in the autumn so that it could be left in piles to weather during the winter frosts, being turned over occasionally. Dobson states that between one-and-three-quarters and two cubic yards, according to the nature of the clay, would produce a thousand bricks.[13]

By 1850 supplies of the pure brickearth, the malm, had almost been used up and so it was more and more frequently necessary to resort to an artificial mixture by adding chalk and a small amount of natural malm to the clay. It was by no means unusual elsewhere in the country to add things to the clay to improve it but the elaborate

lengths to which the makers of London stocks went was unique. The chalk had to be brought on to site (Kent was fortunate in this respect since the chalk and clay occurred in close proximity, whereas in London the chalk often had to be brought in by barge) and ground up in a horse-powered chalk mill. This consisted of a circular trough in which the chalk was ground by two heavy wheels with spiked tyres. Water was pumped into the trough and as the chalk was ground into a pulp it was passed by means of a chute into the clay-washing mill. This was similar to the chalk mill but much larger. In its trough the natural malm was mixed with the chalk pulp, then cut and stirred by knives and harrows moved round by two horses. When reduced to the consistency of cream the whole mixture was passed off through a brass grating into the troughs or shoots, and conducted to the ordinary clay heaped up to receive it. This was arranged in special pits, known as washbacks, fitted with simple sluices. These were left to settle for a month or more until the mixture was solid enough to bear a man walking on top of it. As it settled the water would be drained off from time to time via the sluices.[14]

At this stage *soiling* — the addition of 'Spanish', soil, town ash, or rough stuff (that is the domestic rubbish from London which contained a large amount of ash) — would take place, and was another unique feature of London stock brickmaking. In 1714 the Company of Bricklayers and Tilers said 'the practice of using ashes commonly called Spanish in making bricks begun about forty years since, occasioned by diging up several fields contiguous to the city after the great fire which fields having ben much dunged with ashes it was observed the bricks made with earth in those fields would be sufficiently burned with one half of the coles commonly used'.[15] At about the same date the Surveyors to the Commissioners for the Queen Anne Churches estimated that whereas bricks without Spanish would cost fourteen shillings per thousand, if six loads of Spanish were allowed per 100,000 bricks, the price would fall to twelve shillings and sixpence per thousand.[16] Unfortunately the temptation for brickmakers to add rather too much rubbish and produce poor quality or defective bricks sometimes proved irresistible, as the Surveyors frequently found.[17] As indicated the addition of Spanish saved on fuel cost and also ensured that the bricks were thoroughly burnt right through. According to Dobson about thirty-five chaldrons of soil (that is roughly about forty-four cubic yards) were required to produce every 100,000 bricks.[18] The rubbish would be sieved and only the smaller particles would be used for soiling.[19] The soil was simply laid on as a layer on top of the solidified washback. London's rubbish was therefore a marketable commodity and there were stringent regulations in the metropolis to prevent householders making use of their domestic ashes, which were collected by people who contracted with the parish authorities for this privilege.[20] London rubbish was also used in the Kent and Essex brickworks, providing the barges with a useful two-way voyage, downstream with a load of rubbish and back upstream with a cargo of bricks.[21]

Actual brickmaking would commence in April and continue through the spring and summer into the autumn. The prepared clay would be further tempered by turning it over by spade, at the same time making sure that the ashes were sufficiently mixed in with clay, and water would be added to give the mixture the right consistency. The tempered clay would then be passed through the pug-mill, the purpose being to get the clay to the right dough-like consistency.[22] The pug-mill, again horse-operated, came into use for brickmaking in the late seventeenth century[23] and ensured that the clay was better broken down and mixed together than as previously, when it had been simply stirred with spades and trampled by feet. The pug-mill resembled a very large bucket made either of wood or metal. Inside at the centre was a revolving vertical shaft, to which were attached horizontal knives inclined so that the clay was slowly forced downwards by their motion; there were also cross-knives to help cut the clay and break up any large lumps. Clay tipped in at the top would emerge at the bottom in a state ready for moulding into bricks. It is said that a horse working a ten-hour day would grind twelve and a half cubic yards of clay, sufficient to make about 6,250 bricks.[24] In the making of bricks other than stocks, it would have been during pugging that additions such as sand or chalk, or even the mixing of two types of clay, would have taken place. It was at this stage also that some impurities could be got rid of.

The moulding stool used in the London area was rather different from that used elsewhere. It had a rim at each end to keep the moulding sand from falling off and was provided with a stock

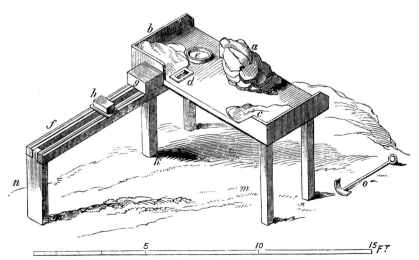

Figure 1. Moulding Stool as used in the London area, *c.* 1850.

    (a) Lump of pugged clay
    (b) Moulder's sand
    (c) Clot-moulder's sand
    (d) Stock board
    (e) Water tub
    (f) *Page*
    (g) Pallets ready for use
    (h) Newly moulded brick
    (k) Moulder's position
    (m) Clot-moulder's position
    (n) Taking-off boy's position
    (o) *Cuckhold*

(From Dobson, Part II, 1850, p. 16.)

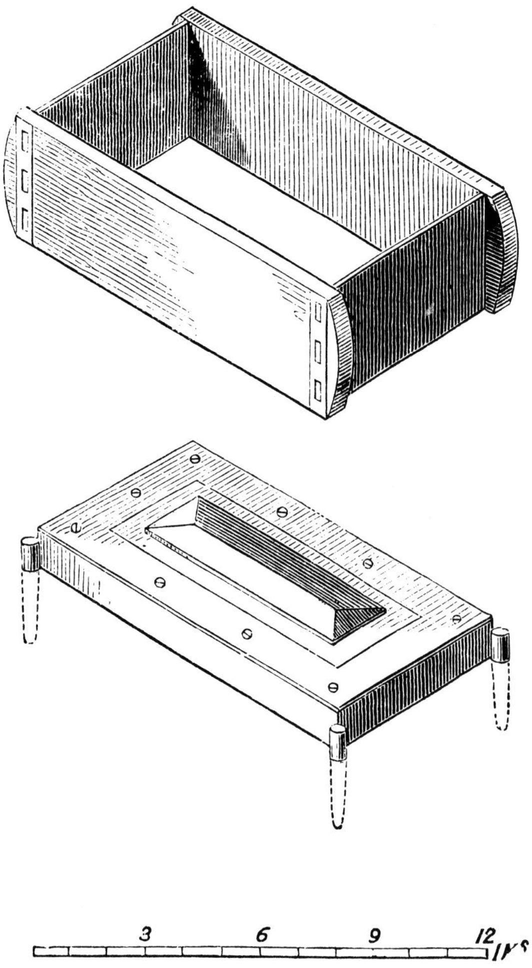

Figure 2. Brick mould (above), with stock board (below). (From Dobson, Part II, 1850, p. 17.)

board which formed a temporary base to the brick mould during actual moulding. The stock board was of wood, plated with iron round the upper edge, and made to fit easily into the mould. It was fastened by iron pins to the stool and these pins could be adjusted to alter the thickness of brick being moulded. A kick, that is a rectangular piece of wood, of the requisite size and shape could be fitted to the top of the stock board to produce a frog, or indentation, in the top of the brick.[25] Incidentally the frog was introduced about 1690 and provided a key for the mortar, while also lightening the weight of the brick.[26]

The London moulding stool was also fitted with a page, formed with two rods of three-eighths inch iron, nailed down at each end to the wooden rails on which they rested. The page allowed raw bricks to be slid more easily by the moulder to the point where they would be picked up by the taking-off boy.[27]

The actual mould, which is simply a four-sided box with no top or bottom, was originally made of wood, but by the mid-nineteenth century was more frequently made of sheet-iron, in four pieces riveted together at the corners and strengthened along the sides with wood.[28] Elsewhere it was common to line the moulds with brass,[29] while today moulds in light alloy may be used. In making the mould allowance has to be made for shrinkage of the brick during firing; since the amount of shrinkage will vary from clay to clay, brick moulds have to be individually made. It should be added that in the Victorian period much of the sand used for brick moulding in London came from Woolwich,[30] while many of the Kent and Essex works drew their sand from Leigh in the latter county.[31]

Moulding was carried out by a team of six, sometimes all members of the same family, and including women and children. A supply of the tempered clay was brought from the pug-mill to the moulding stool by the feeder using a special tool called a cuckhold[32] or else the same three-pronged fork/shovel as used for the digging might be employed. At the stool the clot-moulder, often a woman, sprinkled the stool with dry sand, took a clot or lump of clay, kneaded and roughly worked it into the shape of a brick, and passed it to the moulder standing on his or her left. The moulder having sprinkled sand on the stock board, and dashed the mould into the sand heap on his left hand, placed the mould on the stock board and hurled the clot forcibly into it, pressing it with his fingers to force the clay firmly into the corners of the mould. He would then strike off any superfluous clay with a well-watered strike. The strike was simply a smooth piece of wood about ten inches long and half an inch thick. Alternatively a bow might be used, a curved piece of wood with a

Ia. Brooks's Club, St James's Street (1776–8), from north-east.

Ib. Westminster Cathedral (1895–1903), from the south-east.

Ic. Luton grey bricks from Bedfordshire: former Congregational Church, Lyndhurst Road, Hampstead (1883–4).

Id. Rubbed red-brick dressings: Queen Anne's Gate, Westminster (*c.* 1704).

IIa. Suffolk white bricks: Brooks's Club, St James's Street (1776–8).

IIb. Purple-coloured London stock bricks: Service Wing, Kenwood (1793–6).

IIc. Handmade London stock bricks on left, 1880s; machine-made stocks on right, 1960s: Peabody Clerkenwell Estate, Farringdon Lane.

IId. Beart's patent white gault bricks from Arlesey, Bedfordshire: Farringdon (Thameslink) Station (1860–3).

IIe. Hard red machine-made Ibstock bricks from Leicestershire: University College Hospital, Gower Street.

IIf. Two-inch bricks by Thomas Lawrence and Sons from Wokingham, Berkshire: Westminster Cathedral (1895–1903).

string or wire fixed tautly across it. The moulded brick, still in its mould, was then lifted off the stock board and turned out upon a wooden pallet. This was a wooden board, three-quarters of an inch thick, the exact width of the brickmould, but three-quarters of an inch longer. Each moulder required three sets of pallets, there being twenty-six pallets in each set. A moulding team might make about five thousand bricks during a twelve-hour working day, though this quantity was often exceeded.[33]

The raw brick was removed from the page by the taking-off boy and placed on a hack barrow; when the latter was loaded, dry sand was sprinkled over the bricks, and they were carefully wheeled to the hack ground. Here they were unloaded, a spare pallet being placed on one of the bricks so that it could be carried between two pallets and carefully set up edgeways in the hack, and so on until all twenty-six bricks had been unloaded. Three barrows were used, so that while one was being unloaded at the hack and another was being loaded at the moulding stool, the third was in transit between the two. This meant two men were required for wheeling and hacking, and these completed the six members of the moulding team.

The hacks were set up two bricks in width, with the bricks being set slant-wise rather than at right-angles to the length of the hack. Sufficient time had to be allowed for one row of bricks to be dry enough to stand the weight of another row on top of it and eventually the hacks might be stacked eight to ten rows high. Straw or reeds had to be

ready to cover up the drying bricks as necessary to protect them from frost, rain, or excessive sun.[34] In the later nineteenth and early twentieth century, wooden boards with louvres which would be opened or shut were often used to protect the hacks.[35] When half dry the bricks were moved further apart or 'scintled' to allow air to pass more freely around them. Drying might take from three to six weeks according to the weather.

Another way in which the manufacture of London stocks differed from that of most other bricks was in the absence of kilns. The stocks were simply burnt in a temporary clamp. Edward Dobson, in his great mid nineteenth-century treatise on brickmaking, writes:

The process of clamping requires great skill, and its practical details are little understood, except by the workmen engaged in this part of the manufacture. Scarcely any two clamps are built exactly alike, the differences in the methods employed arising from the greater skill or carelessness of the workmen, and local circumstances.[36]

Certainly the setting up of a clamp, as described by Dobson, was a complicated and skilled job. A base of burnt bricks might be provided and fire holes — known as live holes — had to be formed towards the bottom in order to start the firing and provide some slight control over the rate of firing. The clamp would then be built up with raw bricks, starting with a central stack battered on both sides; then further stacks, known as 'necks', were added, the raw bricks being stacked on edge and laid alternately as headers and stretchers, with a layer of breeze between each course and with

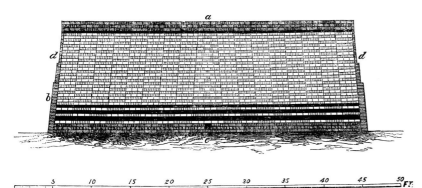

Figure 3. Longitudinal section through a brick clamp. (From Dobson, Part II, p. 28.)

rather more breeze being used in the bottom four layers. The breeze consisted of the large bits of 'Spanish' or rubbish left after sieving.[37] Both the ends and the sides of the clamp were battered. This battering was to stop any tendency for the clamp to topple outwards during firing and cooling. The outsides of the clamp, including the top, were covered over with previously burnt bricks.

Generally fire holes were needed about every seven necks or so; to start the firing, faggots were placed in the holes and lighted. The fire was kept going for about a day and then extinguished. The mouths of the live holes would be stopped up with bricks and plastered over with clay. Firing would of course continue for some considerable time after this and then the clamp would have to be left to cool down before it could be unloaded. In an emergency firing might be completed in two or three weeks, but otherwise it might take up to six weeks, with weather conditions (particularly the amount of damp and the state of the wind) having an effect on the time and the rate of firing. However, the brickmakers themselves had very little control over the firing process. Bricks at the outer edges would be underburnt and were known as samels, burnovers, or shuffs, and would have to be refired the next time. Bricks at the bottom, nearest the fire holes would tend to be overburnt and might even melt and fuse together into clinkers or burrs; these were of little use other than broken up to make the 'crazy-paving'-style brick rubble garden walls to be found around London and the Home Counties.

It should be emphasised that the way in which each and every stage of the brickmaking process was carried out, from the choice of the clay to be used through to the way in which the brick was fired and its position in the kiln, could have a vital effect on the appearance and quality of the finished brick. Hence the many different grades and types of London Stock bricks. Dobson lists for the better work Cutters, Malms, Seconds, Paviours, Pickings, Rough Paviours, Washed Stocks; for Commons he refers to Grey Stocks, Rough Stocks, and Grizzles; while the inferior

bricks include Place Bricks, Shuffs, Burrs or Clinkers, and Bats.[38] Nevertheless terms and grades tended to differ from one brickmaker to another and there was no standard terminology. However, in the later period there seem to have been six main qualities of stock brick, described at Sittingbourne in the 1920s and 1930s as First Hard Stocks, Second Hard Stocks, Mild Stocks, Commons, Picked Roughs, and Roughs.[39] In concluding this brief account of the making of the London stock it remains only to say that it has the fortuituous advantage that it hardens with age and in reaction to the polluted London atmosphere.[40] Also the pock marks left after the Spanish or rough stuff have burnt away leave a porous brick which absorbs moisture but does not retain it and so is not subject to frost damage.[41]

In the eighteenth and nineteenth centuries brickworks, often very temporary in nature, could be found dotted all about London. In the early nineteenth century the centres of brickmaking in south London were Kennington, Walworth, Camberwell, and Battersea. However, the clay on the Surrey side was considered to be less suited to brickmaking than the Middlesex side (amongst other things it contained too much flinty sand).[42] Thus it was that all the brickmakers visited by Dobson in preparing his great study and which were said to include those of the principal London makers, were all in north London, in an arc north of St Pancras, between Finchley and Hackney.[43] Notting Hill and Islington were particularly notable or notorious centres in the nineteenth century.[44] By the mid-century some of the older, inner areas of brick manufacture, such as Fulham and Hammersmith, were beginning to decline, though they were still of some significance;[45] while, as London expanded, outer brickmaking centres like Enfield and Edmonton were developing in importance — at Edmonton, for example, the number of brickmakers rose from 66 in 1851 to 115 in 1861.[46]

Bricks sell relatively cheaply but they are inordinately heavy so that the cost of road transport, certainly in the days of horse-drawn carts and wagons, was proportionately high. In the early nineteenth century it was calculated that to transport bricks a mile by road would increase the cost per thousand by two per cent, and if the distance was extended to five and a half miles the same cost would be increased by forty-one per cent.[47] There was therefore the strongest economic incentive generally to get bricks from the nearest possible source to a building site. This might be the case in London not only for housing, but also for major engineering projects, such as docks and railways, which in any case involved large-scale excavation of the London Clay, and very often the dock and railway companies would set up special brickworks on their own land to exploit this clay and provide at least a proportion of the bricks they required.[48]

Nevertheless there were at least three factors which meant that the capital tended from an earlier period than elsewhere to import bricks from outside. These were first that London was very well served by water transport, initially navigable rivers and from the second half of the eighteenth century canals; secondly, that London as the centre of fashion often required bricks of a particular type, colour, or quality; and thirdly, that the sheer demand for bricks in London could not always be met by local works. In practice, of course, these factors were interrelated, as some specific instances will show. In the Georgian period the softer red bricks required for rubbed brick dressings usually came from elsewhere, from Kent,[49] Sussex,[50] or down the Thames from Windsor.[51] White brick of a particularly good quality, its whiteness enhanced by dipping it in slaked lime, could be brought from Suffolk along rivers such as the Stour and then round the coast to the Thames.[52] The architect, Henry Holland, was largely responsible for a brief fashion for Suffolk whites in the later eighteenth century and used them for Brooks's Club in St James's Street (1776–8),[53] as well as no doubt inspiring George Saunders to employ them for the wings added to Kenwood (1793–6).[54] (Holland also used white brick and mathematical tiles from Exbury, Hampshire in some of his work, including his own house in Sloane Place and the Theatre Royal,

Drury Lane, both no longer existing).[55] By the 1860s Suffolk whites were again in vogue, albeit at a slightly lower social level and were widely used in the new terraces being built in South Kensington.[56]

As, from about 1800, London began to expand rapidly, not only physically and economically, but also in terms of population,[57] so increasing numbers of London stocks were brought into the capital from brickworks dotted along the Essex and Kent banks of the Thames and its tributaries.[58] In Kent the stock brickworks were concentrated along the Medway and the Swale at Halstow, Rainham, Milton, Conyer, Faversham, and most importantly Sittingbourne, while closer to London there was Crayford.[59] On the Essex side the main centres were Ilford, Rainham, Dagenham, Grays Thurrock, Pitsea, and more especially around Southend at Eastwood, Prittlewell, Southchurch, and the Shoeburys.[60]

The opening of the first section of the Grand Junction Canal in 1794, and of its Paddington Branch in 1801, led to many brickfields, often served by their own short branch, springing up along the line of the canal.[61] This was especially true of the area near Uxbridge and Hillingdon — in the vicinity of West Drayton, Hayes, and Southall — where in the mid-1860s there were some twenty-four brickfields along about seven or eight miles of canal.[62] The brick in this area was referred to generically as 'Cowley greys' or 'Cowley stocks' and was considered one of the best types of stock brick for use in London,[63] and, like Suffolk brick, was considered of sufficient quality to face the fashionable houses of Victorian South Kensington.[64] London stocks or 'malms' of an equal quality were produced during the first half of the nineteenth century at Cheshunt in south Hertfordshire, on the Lea Navigation,[65] while later in the century, after the opening of the Slough branch of the Grand Junction Canal in 1882, London stocks were also produced in Buckinghamshire, in the Iver and Langley areas.[66] Water transport was particularly suited to transport heavy commodities such as bricks quite cheaply and a Thames sailing barge could carry a

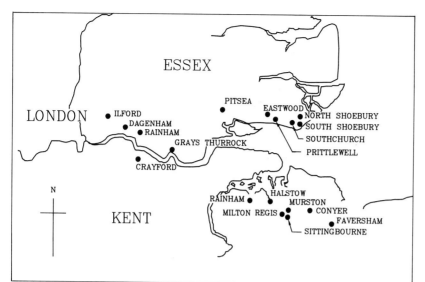

Figure 4. Map of the main centres of stock brickmaking along the River Thames in Kent and Essex, during the later nineteenth and early twentieth centuries.

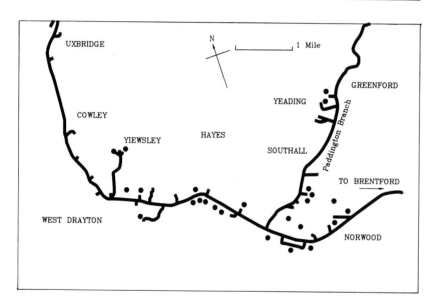

Figure 5. Map of brickworks along the Grand Junction Canal in the Uxbridge and Hillingdon area, *c.* 1865. (Based on O.S. 25- and 6-inch maps, 1st ed., 1864–8.)

load of forty to fifty thousand bricks, while the smaller canal barges might take some thirty to thirty-two thousand bricks at a time.[67] Thus before the coming of the railways large numbers of bricks were already being brought into London.

Otherwise the effect of industrialisation on brickmaking for London was in many instances very little. Brickmaking was generally a small-scale, localised, short-term activity, often carried on by those who regarded themselves chiefly as farmers, builders, etc. In the handmade methods, just described, no buildings were required for

manufacturing and, according to Dobson, in the mid-nineteenth century the equipment would cost under one hundred pounds, with the chalk and clay mills representing by far the greater part of the costs.[68] There was often therefore little incentive or capital available to invest in mechanisation. So in many brickworks traditional handmade methods continued to be used almost unchanged well into the present century. This was especially true in the manufacture of London stocks, which were not very suited to mechanisation, and also of brickworks in the south and south-east of England generally, where in 1937 298 out of 365 works used the full-plastic or handmade method of brickmaking and only sixty-seven used mechanised techniques of moulding or pressing.[69] In 1981 London stocks were still being burnt in a clamp, albeit fired by natural gas, at Murston Works, Sittingbourne.[70]

Elsewhere, however, new brickmaking machines, new and improved types of kilns, together with the development of a national railway system, meant new types of clay could be exploited for bricks and the products transported easily and relatively cheaply to London or anywhere else in the country.

In the 1830s and 1840s brickmaking machines — that is devices that shaped the brick mechanically — were developed, both of the extrusion and press types. In an extrusion machine, when fully developed, the clay was forced by a piston or screw between knives and then rollers, and finally through an aperture with the exact profile of the brick being produced, so that the clay emerged in a continuous mass, rather like toothpaste out of a tube; this could then be automatically cut by a series of wires mounted on a frame, which would come down and chop the continuous mass into individual bricks, which were then described as wire-cuts. Alternatively a machine which pressed the brick into shape might be used, the clay being used in a much drier state and being forced into a metal mould under pressure and pressed (known as the stiff-plastic method).[71] In comparison with handmade bricks, machine bricks have smoother faces, sharper edges ('arrises'), and are more uniform in size.

Machines allowed many more types of clay to be used for brickmaking, especially the harder carbonaceous clays of the Midlands, the north-west, and north Wales, which had proved too intractable for hand moulding. So mechanisation allowed the exploitation of the Keuper Marls of the Triassic system found around Birmingham, Nottingham, Derbyshire, and Leicestershire and which produced hard red bricks such as Ibstocks; and of the hard shales in the Coal Measures both of the Triassic system in Lancashire, Yorkshire,

north Staffordshire, and north Wales, producing very red bricks like the notorious Accrington 'Bloods' and the rather more acceptable reds of Ruabon and Wrexham; and of the Carboniferous system in Staffordshire which, when oxygen was gradually reduced during firing, produced Staffordshire blues, an engineering brick soon to be found in use all over the country. Later in the nineteenth century it was brick presses which allowed the exploitation of the Lower Oxford Clay and the production of the all-conquering Fletton bricks.

The repeal of the Brick Tax in 1850[72] gave both an impetus to the production and improvement of brick machines and also the incentive for certain brickmakers to invest in large-scale production aimed specifically at the London market. An example of this is the works set up at Burham on the Medway in Kent in 1852 by the most famous of all London builders, Thomas Cubitt, at a cost of £54,000. Here the bricks were made by machine, the wash and pug-mills being operated by steam engine, while the clay and bricks were conveyed about the works and to the adjacent river wharf on an internal railway system.[73]

Similarly, some thirty-six miles to the north of London, following the opening of the Great Northern Railway from York to London, Robert Beart of Godmanchester in 1852 established at Arlesey in Bedfordshire what was described at the time as 'an immense works' using steam power to guide the clay and force it into brick machines, while the raw bricks were cured within twenty-four hours, using steam drying stoves. The works had its own siding off the main line and Beart's had an office and depot at King's Cross — such offices and depots in London became essential for any provincial brickmaker wishing to make a significant impact on the London market. By 1858 annual production at Arlesey was eight million bricks and a million agricultural drainage pipes. Beart's produced yellow or white gault bricks, many of them of a patent type with twenty-one or twenty-four perforations, which allowed the bricks to be burnt through more thoroughly and permitted the moisture to escape during firing without fissures. Just how important the firm's London market was is demonstrated by an advertisement of the early twentieth century, while in the 1870s in fashionable South Kensington the Alexander Estate specified that either Beart's patent or Suffolk gault bricks were to be used for new housing on the estate.[74]

The various architectural fashions and movements of the Victorian period — the desire for the sheer modernity given by machine-finished products, the writings of Ruskin on decoration, the fashion for polychromy, the Queen Anne Revival, the Vernacular Revival, and the Arts and Crafts Movement led by William Morris — all encouraged the use of brick, but in very different ways and often using different types of brick. Although still used in large quantities in London the London stock largely ceased to be acceptable in fashionable artistic circles — George Edmund Street dismissed them as 'those detestable-looking dirty yellow bricks in which London so much rejoices'.[75] Instead bricks of almost every colour and texture might be brought in by train and boat from the four points of the compass. Butterfield, though largely using stock bricks, incorporates Staffordshire Blues and red Suffolk bricks from Ballingdon near Sudbury in his polychromatic treatment of St Augustine's Church, Queen's Gate, South Kensington.[76] Fareham Reds from Hampshire supplied just the right even colour and texture for the fastidious tastes of Prince Albert and Henry Cole to go with the terracotta of the South Kensington buildings, such as the Albert Hall and the South Kensington Museum.[77] St Pancras Station and the Midland Hotel are built of Gripper's patent bricks brought at Gilbert Scott's insistence from Nottingham in spite of their greater cost.[78] Luton Greys, made also in fact in adjacent parts of south Bedfordshire, Buckinghamshire, and Hertfordshire — a lovely plum-coloured brick lightly vitrified to give a silvery-grey glaze — were used in two adjacent churches in Hampstead: St Stephen's, Rosslyn Hill, by Teulon and the Congregational Church in Lyndhurst Road by Waterhouse.[79] Narrow red bricks from Gibbons of Ipswich can be seen in

Lowther Lodge, Kensington Gore, built between 1873 and 1875.[80] And one could go on almost indefinitely, but just one more example will suffice: Westminster Cathedral, built 1895 to 1903, again is faced in two-inch bricks, but this time made by Thomas Lawrence and Sons at their Wokingham Works in Berkshire.[81] The main shell is of stock brick from Sittingbourne[82] but the cathedral also contains ten million Fletton bricks from Peterborough (though only used for concealed work), the first such major order for this type of brick, and a precursor of what was to come.[83]

The Fletton brick is so called because it was at Fletton, a village near Peterborough, that in 1881 it was first discovered that below the brownish top callow of the Oxford Clay, which can be ten to forty feet in depth, was a shale-like, grey-green clay deposit, known as the 'Knotts', which can be anything from twenty to a hundred feet in depth, though usually it forms a layer about forty-five to fifty feet deep.[84] This clay is peculiarly suited to modern brickmaking. The moisture content being constant, the clay can be crushed into a granular form and then pressed into a brick capable of being fired immediately without any pre-drying. The Knotts also contain combustible materials, mainly shale-oil, which make the bricks almost self-burning and reduce fuel consumption by about two-thirds. The lime content is constant and exactly right to prevent cracking during firing. Finally the clay contains remarkably few impurities.[85]

Large-scale exploitation required not only the use of brick presses and eventually mechanical clay excavators, but most importantly the adoption of multi-chambered kilns of the Hoffman type, so named because they were patented by an Austrian, Friedrich Hoffman, in 1858.[86] These allow continuous firing and some have worked constantly for over fifty years without ever being fully extinguished.[87] The largest kiln at Stewartby in Bedfordshire has no less than eighty chambers, each with a capacity of 76,000 bricks and capable of producing a total of 3,500,000 bricks a week.[88]

By April 1889 *The Builder* was reporting that 156,000 bricks were being dispatched daily from Fletton.[89] From the late 1890s further Fletton works were opened in Bedfordshire and Buckinghamshire, all of course associated with the Oxford Clay and all adjacent to railway lines.[90] The Fletton industry from the first had its eyes almost wholly fixed on the London market and was dependent on it;[91] indeed London was the only place where Flettons could undercut the price of local bricks, and in the 1890s and early 1900s Flettons were instrumental in forcing down the price of London stocks.[92] By 1914 the price of Fletton commons in London was twenty-two shillings and sixpence a thousand, compared with London stock commons at twenty-eight shillings and sixpence. By 1938 the gap had widened, with Flettons at forty-six shillings and threepence a thousand, while Stocks were almost twice as expensive at eighty-eight shillings, and this gap has continued.[93]

In 1892, according to *The British Clay-Worker*,[94] London required on average eight hundred million bricks a year, which were supplied approximately as follows:

Sittingbourne Yards	250,000,000
London Yards	150,000,000
Peterborough and other Great Northern Railway Yards [i.e. Fletton bricks]	100,000,000
Shoeburyness and Sheerness	100,000,000
Cowley and Grand Junction Canal	100,000,000
Yards on Great Eastern Railway generally	100,000,000

And the Fletton share of the London market was to increase.[95] However, the impact of Flettons is not so immediately visible as the figures might suggest because until 1922 when the first Fletton facing bricks, Rustics, were produced, Flettons were only available as commons.[96]

Today London's historic brick buildings give ample testimony to the truth of Wren's words about the durability of the material. Bricks are no longer manufactured in London but with a recent return by many architects to bricks as a facing material, their use in the capital is probably as great as ever and is likely to continue in the foreseeable future.

BIBLIOGRAPHY

Brunskill, Ronald, and Clifton Taylor, Alec, *English Brickwork*, Ward Lock (London, 1977).

Dobson, Edward, *A Rudimentary Treatise on the Manufacture of Bricks and Tiles*, John Weale (London, 1850). (13 subsequent editions to 1936; facsimile of 1850 edition, edited by Francis Celoria, published by George Street Press, Stafford, 1971, as *Journal of Ceramic History No. 5*.)

Hillier, Richard, *Clay that Burns: A History of the Fletton Brick Industry*, London Brick Company Ltd (London, 1981).

Lloyd, Nathaniel, *A History of English Brickwork*, H. Greville Montgomery (London, 1925). (This edition reprinted by The Antique Collectors' Club, Woodbridge, 1983.)

Woodforde, John. *Bricks to Build a House*, Routledge and Kegan Paul (London, 1976).

SOME BRICK BUILDINGS IN LONDON AT WHICH TO LOOK

1. Orangery, Kensington Palace (1704, fine brickwork of the Wren School, with much rubbed red brickwork).
2. Nos. 5–25, 14–32 Queen Anne's Gate, Westminster (*c.* 1704, rubbed red brick dressings).
3. Brooks's Club, St James's Street, Westminster (1777–8, Suffolk white brick).
4. Stable Block to Kenwood (1797, earthy, purplish London stock brick).
5. Peabody Estate, Farringdon Lane (later nineteenth century, handmade yellow London stock brick with bands of Beart's patent Arlesey white gault brick, together with machine-made yellow stocks for the twentieth-century addition to the south).
6. St Augustine's Church, Queen's Gate, Kensington (1865–71, yellow London stock brick, embellished with red brick from Ballingdon, Suffolk, blue Staffordshire brick, and Pether's patent moulded brick).
7. Albert Hall, Kensington Gore (1867–71, Fareham red brick from Hampshire).
8. St Pancras Station (1868–74, Gripper's patent machine-made red bricks from Nottingham).
9. Former Congregational Church, Lyndhurst Road, Hampstead (1883–4, Luton 'grey' brick from Bedfordshire).
10. Westminster Cathedral (1895–1903, faced in two-inch red bricks from Wokingham, Berkshire).

NOTES

[1] *The Wren Society* IX (1932), 16.
[2] *Survey of London* 5 (1914), 42–58, plates 16–20; 36 (1970), 64–97.
[3] *The British Architect* XVIII (1 Dec. 1882), 574.

[4] John Houghton, *A Collection of Letters For the Improvement of Husbandry & Trade* II (1683), 186–7. Richard Neve, *The City and Country Purchaser and Builder's Dictionary*, 2nd ed. (1726), 42–4. Batty Langley, *The London Prices of Bricklayer's Materials and Works* (1749 ed.) 1 and 2. Isaac Ware, *The Complete Body of Architecture* (1756), 59.

[5] Lambeth Palace Library MS 2723 ff. 21v-22 (13 May 1714).

[6] Ian Smalley, 'The nature of Brickearth and the location of early brick buildings in Britain', *British Brick Society, Information No. 41* (Feb. 1987), 4–11.

[7] Joseph Moxon, *Mechanick Exercises* (1682, 1703 ed.), 239.

[8] Edward Dobson, *A Rudimentary Treatise on the Manufacture of Bricks and Tiles*, Part II (1850), 2, 21.

[9] *Victoria County History of Kent* III (1932), 394. D. G. R. Bonnell and B. Butterworth, *Clay Building Bricks of the United Kingdom*, National Brick Advisory Council, Paper Five (1950), 15.

[10] Dobson, *op. cit.*, II, 3–4.

[11] Richard-Hugh Perks, *George Bargebrick Esquire* (1981), 51.

[12] *Ibid.*, 25.

[13] Dobson, *op. eit.*, II, 21.

[14] *Ibid.*, 2, 5, 7, 21–2, 41, 47–8.

[15] Lambeth Palace Library MS 2723, ff. 21v–22 (13 May 1714). See also John Houghton, *Husbandry and Trade Improv'd* (revised and corrected ed. 1727), I, No. LXVIII (1 Dec. 1693), 191; No. LXIX (8 Dec. 1693), 192–3; No. LXXIII (22 Dec. 1693), 197.

[16] Lambeth Palace Library MS 2690, 134 (30 Dec. 1713).

[17] Lambeth Palace Library MS 2713, f. 15 (23 March 1715); MS 2715, f. 183 (9 Nov. 1713); MS 2717, f. 83 (10 Dec. 1713); MS 2723, f. 35 (6 April 1715).

[18] Dobson, *op. cit.*, II, 4, 22.

[19] Houghton, *op. cit.*, No. LXIX (8 Dec. 1693), 192.

[20] Dobson, *op. cit.*, II, 22, 42.

[21] Perks, *op. cit.*, 33, 47.

[22] Dobson, *op. cit.*, II, 23, 48–9.

[23] John Woodforde, *Bricks to Build a House* (1976), 61.

[24] Dobson, *op. cit.*, II, 23.

[25] *Ibid.*, 7–18, 49.

[26] L. S. Harley, 'A Typology of Brick', *The Journal of the British Archaeological Association*, 3rd series, XXXVII (1974), 80.

[27] Dobson, *op. cit.*, II, 9.

[28] *Ibid.*, 17, 49.

[29] Dobson, *op. cit.*, Part I, Fig. 7 and p. 94.

[30] Dobson, *op. cit.*, II, 4, 41–2.

[31] Perks, *op. cit.*, 25.

[32] Dobson, *op. cit.*, II, 7.

[33] *Ibid.*, 10, 18, 23–4.

[34] *Ibid.*, 24–5.

[35] Perks, *op. cit.*, 28, 29.

[36] Dobson, *op. cit.*, II, 25–6.

[37] Graham West, 'The Former Brickmaking Industry of Langley, Buckinghamshire', *News Bulletin of the Middle Thames Archaeological and Historical Society* 1, No. 5 (Spring 1965), 7.

[38] Dobson, *op. cit.*, II, 26–38, 50.

[39] Perks, *op. cit.*, 54–5.

[40] *Ibid.*, 29.

[41] Bonnell and Butterworth, *op. cit.*, 19–21.

[42] *Victoria County History of Surrey* II (1905), 281.

[43] Dobson, *op. cit.*, 40–1.

[44] Florence M. Gladstone and Ashley Barker, *Notting Hill in Bygone Days* (1969), 66–70, 133–4. Hermione Hobhouse, *Thomas Cubitt, Master Builder* (1971), 302, 345–6. *Survey of London*, 37 (1973), 16.

[45] Rev. Daniel Lysons, *Environs of London* II, 2nd ed. (1792), Part I, 261, 265. Thomas Faulkner, *The History and Antiquities of the Parish of Hammersmith* (1839), 46–9. C. J. Fèret, *Fulham Old and New* III (1900), 3. Philip D. Whitting (ed.), *A History of Hammersmith* (1965), 12, 89, 125, 185. Dorothy Stroud, *Henry Holland: His Life and Architecture* (1966), 17–18.

[46] *Industrial Archaeology in Enfield*, Enfield Archaeological Society Research Paper No. 2 (1971), 23.

[47] Alan Cox, *Survey of Bedfordshire: Brickmaking, A History and Gazetteer* (1979), 178.

[48] Museum of London (Museum in Docklands Project), East India Dock Company Minute Book A, 188–9, 194–7, 222, 247–8, 258–61, 361; Minute Book B, 28; West India Dock Company Minute Book 297, pp. 95–102, 191, 279, 365, 371; Minute Book 301, pp. 371, 449, 478; Minute Book 303, ff. 33, 35, 38–40, 45–53, 73, 191, 193, 202. *The Times*, 24 Aug. 1866, p. 9 b-c. *Survey of London*, 42 (1986), 328.

[49] Joseph Moxon, *Mechanick Exercises* (1682, 1703 ed.), 239.

[50] Dan Cruikshank and Peter Wyld, *London: The Art of Georgian Building* (1975), 178.

[51] Sir John Summerson, *Georgian London* (revised ed. 1962), 80. 'The Story of Brick' IX, *Harrison Mayer Monthly Bulletin for the Ceramic Industry* (June/July 1976), no pagination.

[52] Information from Mr Peter Minter of Bulmer Brick and Tile Company.

[53] Stroud, *op. cit.*, 13, 50–2, 132 (but she does not specifically state that the bricks for Brooks's Club came from Suffolk).

[54] Sir John Summerson, *The Iveagh Bequest, Kenwood: A Short Account of its History and Architecture* (1967, revised ed. 1988), 10, 15.

[55] Stroud, *op. cit.*, 39, 46, 119.

[56] *Survey of London* 42 (1986), 124, 170, 378n.

[57] Sir John Summerson, *Georgian London* (revised ed. 1962), 25, 258–87. Francis Sheppard, *London 1808–1870: The Infernal Wen* (1971), xv–xx, 1–2, 83–116.

[58] J. M. Preston, *Industrial Medway: an historical survey* (1977), 51.

[59] *Victoria County History of Kent* III (1932), 394.

[60] *Victoria County History of Essex* II (1907), 457.

[61] Carolynne Hearmon, *Uxbridge: A Concise History* (1982), 50–1. Alan H. Faulkner, *The Grand Junction Canal* (1972), 97.

[62] Ordnance Survey 25 and 6 inch maps of the area (1st ed., 1864–68).

[63] *The Builder* 5 (17 April 1847), 177.

[64] *Survey of London* 41 (1983), 77.

[65] Dobson, *op. cit.*, II, 39–40.

[66] Faulkner, *op. cit.*, 200–1.

[67] Perks, *op. cit.*, 31.

[68] *Ibid.*, 43–4.

[69] Marian Bowley, *Innovations in Building Materials* (1960), 62, 172.

[70] Perks, *op. cit.*, 58, 59.

[71] Woodforde, *op. cit.*, 110–17, 120–2.

[72] 13 and 14 Vict., c. 9.

[73] *The Builder* 10 (19 June 1852), 385. Hobhouse, *op. cit.*, 310–15.

[74] Cox, *op. cit.*, 44–5, 100. Bedfordshire County Council: Sites and Monuments Record, SMR 6728. *Survey of London*, 42 (1986), 170.

[75] G. E. Street. *Brick and marble of the Middle Ages* (1855), 278.

[76] Paul Thompson, *William Butterfield* (1971), 149. *Survey of London* 38 (1975), 351.

[77] *Survey of London* 38 (1975), 90–1, 121, 189, 198, 237.

[78] Jack Simmons, *St. Pancras Station* (1968), 53.

[79] Neil Burton, *The Church of St. Stephen, Rosslyn Hill, Hampstead*, Greater London Council, Historic Buildings Paper No 1, no date, no pagination. Nikolaus Pevsner, *The Buildings of England: London (except the Cities of London and Westminster)* (1952), 188 (only described here as 'purple brick'). See also Cox, *op. cit.*, 33–4.

[80] *Survey of London* 38 (1975), 330.

[81] Michael Dumbleton, *Brickmaking: A Local Industry* (1978), 8.

[82] Perks, *op. cit.*, 9.

[83] Woodforde, *op. cit.*, 148, 150.

[84] *Ibid.*, 147–9.

[85] Cox, *op. cit.*, 50.

[86] M. D. P. Hammond, 'Brick Kilns: An Illustrated History', *Industrial Archaeology Review* 1, No. 2 (Spring 1977), 181, 185.

[87] Woodforde, *op. cit.*, 120.

[88] London Brick Company Ltd., *Stewartby*, 1974 (duplicated information sheet).

[89] *The Builder* 56 (27 April 1889), 324.

[90] Cox, *op. cit.*, 50–9. Richard Hillier, *Clay that Burns: A History of the Fletton Brick Industry* (1981), 88–90, 92–6.

[91] Hillier, *op. cit.*, 17–18.

[92] Bowley, *op. cit.*, 174–5. Perks, *op. cit.*, 42. Hillier, *op. cit.*, 117–18.

[93] Bowley, *op. cit.*, 177.

[94] *The British Clay-Worker* 1, No. 8 (15 Nov. 1892), 161.

[95] Bowley, *op. cit.*, 181.

[96] Woodforde, *op. cit.*, 157.

STUCCO

by FRANK KELSALL

Augustus at Rome was for building renowned
And of marble he left what of brick he had found.
But is not our Nash, too, a very great master?
He finds us all brick and he leaves us all plaster.

This well-known verse makes the point that no discussion about stucco can leave out the crucial role played by Nash. But the verse would lose its bite if the implication was not also there that stucco was even then (1826) regarded as an inferior material. None of the other materials considered in these papers has had such a bad press: cheap, therefore nasty. It is not that long ago that the seedier parts of London were characterised as Rillington Places in which the stucco is always 'peeling'.

So stucco was under attack even before the moralistic fervour of Pugin, Ruskin, and almost every architectural writer of the later nineteenth and early twentieth centuries. Stucco did not appeal to Gothic revivalists, arts and craftsmen, free Renaissance men or, apparently, anyone else. But, before we look at what positive qualities stucco contributed to the architecture of London, we should look carefully at what stucco was.

Here we have a problem. We all know what a stuccoed house looks like. But such buildings were frequently not referred to by contemporaries as stuccoed. The very words we deal with confuse rather than clarify. Most eighteenth-century handbooks use 'stucco' as a description for internal work, what we would now perhaps call ornamental plasterwork, though the craftsmen, because they were often foreigners or because art historians like to show off their Italian accents, are often called 'stuccatori'. Likewise with the word 'cement' we have problems, for what was patented as Portland cement in 1824 was not what would now be recognised as Portland cement.

We can agree, however, that stucco can be defined as some sort of composition which can be applied to the whole or part of a house front and can be used equally for a plain covering or for running mouldings and forming ornament. The age of stucco, if we may use the phrase, is perhaps the period from 1775 to 1850. During that time four broad types, with many variations, patented and unpatented, within each type, were in use. But long before then a lime and sand mixture was used both for overall covering and for decoration. There was, of course, pargetting in the south-east, render or roughcast in the north and harling in Scotland, long established as vernacular materials. But stucco is essentially a polite material. It appears as a lime/sand mixture on Inigo Jones's buildings at the Queen's Chapel and the Queen's House. It could be used decoratively in artisan mannerist houses such as Swakeleys. It could be used, in the same way as Portland stone, to contrast with fine red brick of the later seventeenth century. And, of course, with the revival of interest in Inigo Jones and Palladio by the English Palladians, it could be use in exact imitation of Italian precedent.

The great problem, of course, is that the English climate is not as friendly to stucco as the Italian and it was probably this which led John Gwynn to remark, in *London and Westminster Improved* (1766) that he wished that the recent repair of St James's had included the stuccoing of the church; 'It is to be lamented that encouragement is not given to some ingenious person to find out a stucco or composition resembling stone, *more*

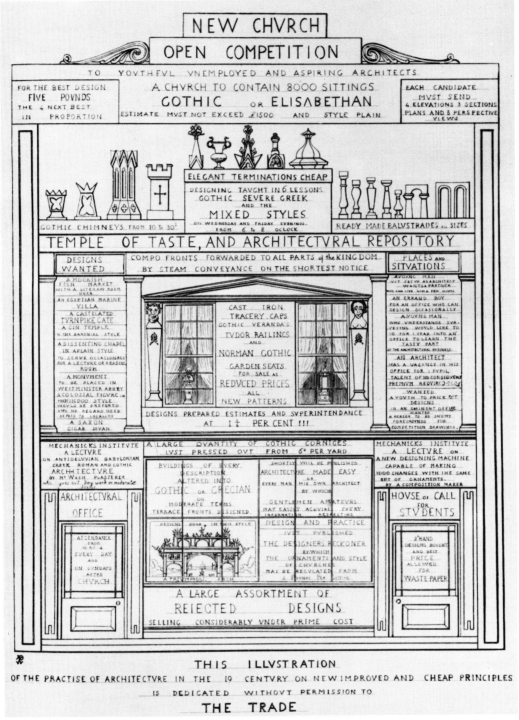

Figure 1. Contrasts was published by A. W. N. Pugin in 1836 to show the superiority of medieval building. Among the current architectural fads satirised in the frontispiece were 'composition fronts'.

durable than the common sort . . .' [my italics]. From this time on stucco is usually thought of as an invented, patented or manufactured product rather than a combination of basic materials (though of course lime itself has to be manufactured). But in our later discussion of patent stucco we should remember that a simple lime/sand stucco was always available.

It may be coincidence that a year before Gwynn's book was published, the Revd David Wark had patented a stucco and that shortly afterwards, when the Adam brothers began the great Adelphi enterprise, they acquired Wark's patent. Wark's composition was used on some buildings in the Adelphi but for ornament, not for overall covering. In 1774, when the Adam brothers bought a new patent stucco, they specifically undertook no longer to produce Wark's stucco.

The stucco which the Adam brothers bought was that invented by the Revd John Liardet a year before. This new composition was mixed up in the vaults beneath the Adelphi and dispatched in barrels to building sites all over London, its suburbs, and the Home Counties. What distinguished Wark's and Liardet's stucco from the common sort was that they were oil based. The specification for Liardet was vague but the crucial ingredient was the boiled linseed oil, not water, which made the composition workable. Perhaps it was thought that oil cement would protect brickwork just as oil paint protected woodwork. For some ten years Liardet's cement was all the rage. It was used, as both general covering and cast decoration, on major houses such as Kenwood. When, in 1778, the owner of Kenwood, Lord Chief Justice Mansfield, found in favour of the

Figure 2. Bedford Square was built under agreements of 1776. References in the lawsuits over Liardet's cement show that it was used there, where the centre pieces of the four sides are stuccoed. Other decoration was in Coade stone. This drawing of 1851 by T. H. Shepherd is one of a pair on the east side.

Adam brothers' patent rights in a trial, it was said that his verdict was given in the hope that it would prolong the life of his stucco which, he declared, had cost him a great deal. Liardet's stucco could be cast into moulds and similar decorative details appear in such places as Woodlands, Blackheath, and Portland Place. But it was principally as an overall stucco that Liardet found favour. By the 1770s there was a much better alternative — Coade stone — for work which could be moulded off-site. But even in a place such as Bedford Square, where Coade stone was used for some detail, Liardet was used as well; we know this from the evidence of John Utterton, a plasterer, who testified to the fact that a capital executed in Liardet fell off.

One of the Adam brothers' clerks of works was John Johnson who shortly afterwards set up practice as an architect. He invented his own stucco or, as the brothers alleged, pirated Liardet's composition, and it was for this breach of patent that Lord Chief Justice Mansfield's services were called upon. Johnson claimed his own stucco to be different — it had ox blood in it — but the court found against him. It was said that Johnson used his stucco at his two houses in New Cavendish Street (nos. 61–3), though it is difficult to see where. But the issues debated in Liardet *versus* Johnson in 1778 very soon became academic. Oil-based stuccoes began to fall off buildings with increasing regularity, to the great financial embarrassment of the Adam brothers who, for instance, had £1,500 damages awarded against them in an action by Earl Stanhope for failed stucco at Chevening. By 1781 Liardet was suing the brothers, his failure to receive any more royalties being, in his belief, on account of their fraudulent conduct.

But it was the stucco itself that was the problem. Liardet himself perhaps realised this for he claimed to have invented a water-stucco. As far as is known it was never made. What was made, however, was a stucco invented by Dr Bryan Higgins, a chemist to whom samples of Liardet's and Johnson's cement had been submitted in the course of the patent action of 1778. Higgins's

cement was taken up by James and Samuel Wyatt and used by them on a few buildings (9 Conduit Street, for example). Water-based cement only became a practical proposition after 1796, as we shall see in a few moments.

But before that we should look briefly at a last example of the use of Liardet's cement which introduces John Nash into the story. Nash began as a speculative builder, converting the corner house in Bloomsbury Square into two houses in the early 1780s and building six new houses behind in Great Russell Street. The whole lot was faced with Liardet's cement, one of the largest uses of the composition and described by the Adam brothers as 'a very great work'. The lack of success of this speculation led to Nash's bankruptcy and disappearance to South Wales whence he was to reappear in London some twenty years later, his appetite for both building speculation and stucco increased rather than diminished by his experience.

But when Nash returned to London the stucco scene was very different. In 1796 the Revd James Parker (yet another clergyman inventor) took out a patent for a cement which soon became known as Parker's Roman Cement. It was made by burning and then grinding nodules found in the Thames estuary by Sheppey. The end product was a hydraulic cement which could be mixed with sand and used for many building purposes, including stucco. By the early nineteenth century it was frequently specified by name and when Nash's proposals for Regent's Park were produced in 1811 he made disparaging remarks about speculative builders and Parker's stucco, ironic in view of his forthcoming extensive involvement with both. A year later he was specifying it for Park Crescent and many other places on the Crown Estate. Much of what we now regard as the best building of the twenty years after Waterloo was in fact executed in stucco.

Parker's fourteen-year patent expired in 1810, though he had by then sold out to yet another of the ubiquitous Wyatts, Charles. Charles Wyatt's extensive supplies of the material to his cousin

James Wyatt led the latter being described at one time as having 'cement influenza'. By 1812 there were another two Roman cement manufacturers in the market and a commercial London directory of 1822–3 lists eleven. Supplies began to come from the area around Harwich as well as from Sheppey. In 1851 it was said that up to 400 boats were employed in dredging the raw materials for Roman cement from the Thames estuary by Walton on the Naze. We have clearly moved a long way from the time when Liardet's cement was mixed up in a couple of vaults underneath the Adelphi.

It was Roman cement which held the dominant share of the stucco market for the first half of the nineteenth century. But other cements were invented, patented, and marketed. Nash specified Hamelin's cement for the United Services Club — one always suspects that he would specify a patent if he could get a rake-off from the patentee — and this was used also at the Athenaeum. Dehl's mastic, another oil-based composition, also sometimes appears, but its application must have been made difficult by disagreements in contemporary handbooks as to how it should be applied, some stating that it should only be used as a fine top coat on a Roman cement base, others stating specifically that it was not to be so used. A patent metallic cement, made from the slag of copper smelting, was used by Sir Robert Smirke on houses on the approach to London Bridge. Some of these compositions had impressive names — Egyptian mastic or Vitruvian cement — but the names had as little connection with historical precedent as the Georgian windows in a modern builder's catalogue.

By the 1830s stucco had created not a dilemma of style but a dilemma of material. When the line of clubs along Pall Mall was extended to the Reform in 1837 Barry's design could have been executed in stucco or stone; the club opted for the stone at an increase in building cost of some ten per cent — an extra £3,500 on £38,000. The dilemma in attitudes can be seen in quotations from two well-used publications: Loudon's *Architectural Magazine* (Vol. 1, 1834) commented on the importance of the plasterer who has sole employment of that material which produces such magical effects on exteriors, Roman cement. In consequence of the discovery of cements of this kind we are now enabled to erect buildings of brick, coated over with this material, which are as handsome as those of stone and much stronger and more durable ... we are enabled to display every kind of architectural form and ornament in many cases at a fifth of the expense that similar ornaments would cost if formed either of moulded bricks or of stone.

Five years later (significantly perhaps Pugin's *Contrasts* with its attack on stucco came in between) Bartholomew's *Specifications* has a chapter entitled 'Of the degradation which the general use of stucco has brought upon architecture and how it has tended to ruin both taste and constructive excellence in English building'. Bartholomew notes that stucco has some proper uses: the tarting up of an old house, too old to be worth more substantial restoration, the building of a short-lived country house which caprice may soon wish to do away with, and the facing of a theatre which is likely to be burnt down or whose owners will probably go bankrupt.

To these three broad types of stucco — the lime/sand mixture, the oil-based composition, and Roman cement — should be added Portland cement, described in 1863 as a 'nine-days wonder' by one correspondent to the *Builder*. As external stucco it was probably of relatively little significance. Although Joseph Aspdin's patent of 1824 is called 'Portland' cement, the process which he used did not produce a material which we would now recognise under that name. The essential feature of Portland cement is the heating of the clay/lime raw material to a temperature that produces clinkering; this seems to have been stumbled on by accident in the 1840s and it took some time for the material to supersede the Roman cements; by that time stucco was a thing of the past. Portland cement has found its principal uses in many other parts of the building process.

Any tour of inner or suburban London will quickly show how stucco could be used for rusticated ground floors, for all-over covering, for

Figures 3 and 4. Two photographs of Calthorpe Street, Grays Inn Road, showing the effect of stucco on minor street architecture. The very plain nos. 2–24 were built under agreement of 1816, the more ornamented nos. 23–43 under agreement of 1843.

architectural articulation and for ornament. It is one of the essential elements in the style which we have come to call rather loosely 'Regency' but which spreads more widely over the late Georgian and early Victorian period.

So far we have looked at stucco applied to new buildings. But some comments — Gwynn in 1766 or Bartholomew in 1839 — show that stucco was regarded as an appropriate material to use in the repair of an old building. Lindsey House, built 1640, was repaired some years ago and pieces of the stucco were examined in detail. It was clear that the original building had contrasted the red brick of the main house with the stone of the pilasters (remember that the Banqueting House also originally had a colour contrast of three differing stones), a contrast now reinstated with paint. But the front had clearly undergone several stages of repair. The original fine jointed brickwork had been repointed, but each repointing damaged the arrises of the bricks; at one time this had been remedied by tuck-pointing. Eventually, perhaps the middle of the eighteenth century, the face of the brickwork was regarded as beyond repair and the whole of the surface was stuccoed. This first quotation in the *Oxford English Dictionary* which uses 'stucco' in the manner treated in this paper is a reference to a proposed stuccoing of the Old Court at Peterhouse in Cambridge in 1754. In 1750 a repairing lease was granted by the Bedford Estate which required the stuccoing of the front of 14 Bloomsbury Square, the first reference I know to that being done to an old building; the house was about eighty years old by then. Such work can radically change the character of a street or a building. Nash's work in Bloomsbury Square was perhaps so comprehensively stuccoed because the corner house, if not the houses behind, was essentially a remodelling of the later seventeenth-century house.

There are two final issues which should be considered. The first is what happened to newly applied stucco. Although some patent compositions claimed not to need painting, it is clear that most stucco was from the beginning intended to be painted. But initially this took the form of colour washing, or, more expensively, frescoing in imitation of stone. In 1813 the plasterer/sculptor Francis Bernasconi was said to be the most distinguished exponent of the art of frescoing Parker's Roman Cement. This was a means of making the stucco, already lined and jointed like ashlar, take on the weathered appearance of stone. The temporary nature of colour washing and expense of frescoing meant that eventually stucco came to be oil-painted. But although there are one or two references in the 1820s and 1830s which suggest that oil painting was used, it seems not to have become general until the 1840s. The glossy white or cream finish to stucco which we now accept as normal was probably unknown to Nash.

The second issue is the relationship between the material and the architecture of which it is so much a part. To those who believe that design follows technology, then the increased availability of stucco from the 1770s may be taken as one contributor to the changes which took place in English architecture at the end of the eighteenth century. But, as far as stucco is concerned, this interpretation is of limited value. Stucco was not in design terms an innovative material; its very essence was imitative. Design was led for the most part by those who could afford to build in stone, and stucco aped their designs, bringing pretensions to architecture to a greatly increased number of buildings. This is not the place to hold a philosophical discussion of when building becomes architecture. But today most people will accept that stucco did much to enliven the London street scene.

BIBLIOGRAPHICAL NOTE

Sources for specific quotations are given in the text. The earliest work to give scientific study to stucco was C. W. Pasley, *Observations on Limes, Calcareous Cements, etc.* (1838). My paper 'Liardet versus Adam' in *Architectural History* 27 (1984) discusses the early oil-based cements while the paper by A. P. Thurston, 'Parker's Roman Cement' in *Transactions of the Newcomen Society* 19 (1938) discusses the introduction of Roman cement. The most significant recent general work is A. J. Francis, *The Cement Industry 1796–1914: A History* (1977).

SHINING THROUGH THE SMOG
Terracotta and Faience

by MICHAEL STRATTON

London became a major architectural testing ground, as it emerged as a world industrial city and the focus of the British Empire. Architects and critics not only judged the capital's buildings according to whether they presented a style appropriate to the modern age but by their materials. Stone, brick, its more heavily moulded counterpart terracotta, and iron were judged by their finish, their ability to carry decoration and to resist fire, and pollution. Each major example of terracotta was evaluated as to whether it marked a step towards a decorative architecture for the cities of the industrial age.

The Victorians believed that their architecture should have 'meaning', expressing the values of wealth and culture which they held so dear. Pure form, the hallmark of Georgian building, meant little to a society anxious to display its prosperity. In 1868 *The Builder* reported on current efforts to replace 'the dead walls and unmeaning windows of the Georgian style of street building'.[1]

The Victorians judged architecture, from town halls to public conveniences, as a barometer of the state of their cities and society. Ornamentation had a direct social function. Books, journals, and art training classes created a broad and articulate awareness of styles, materials, and the sister arts of sculpture and painting.[2] Most educated people could judge, and read meanings into building façades. As they walked on the opposite pavement or rode on an omnibus they could gauge the opulence of apartments in Mayfair by the intricacy of their fenestration, draw inspiration from bas-reliefs on a museum and art school, or be lured by the Baroque corner tower of an 'improved' public house.

Away from Pugin and the Ecclesiologists, mid-Victorian designers came to regard architectural ceramics as ideal media for introducing 'meaning' into a façade. The simplest approach was to emblazon the name of a business or institution in a pediment or gable end. Moulded panels set into wall surfaces carried greater prestige than the painted signs which cluttered most commercial streets. Sculptural representations of activities relevant to the building were welcomed as being more artistic and less blatantly commercial. The terracotta frieze on the Cutler's Hall in London, dating to 1888, gained warm approval: the scenes of workers forging, grinding, and filing 'in such a land as ours must in a sense affect every passer-by, or, we may say, every intelligent observer'. Credit was given to the decorative artist, Benjamin Creswick, who modelled the panels: 'the man who can handle the current interest in our daily life and fix it for us in a permanent decoration makes a stronger appeal to our sympathies than the idealist, however skilled he be'.[3]

The bulk of the bricks and mortar of the Victorian period and the first half of the twentieth century reflected a pragmatic acceptance of the modern world. Most builders and clients were direct beneficiaries of rapid industrial and urban growth. Originality, economy, and the dissemination of Science and Art could all be promoted through a factory-made decorative material such as terracotta. Mass-produced decoration, moulded into Classical or Renaissance forms, would encourage a broad acceptance of cultured values and taste, and a respect for the status quo. This 'improving' philosophy was directly applied through the museum and art school movement, centred on South Kensington. Through the work of the Department of Science and Art, terracotta was adopted as the ideal medium for the teaching of three-dimensional modelling, and was used on museums and art schools erected not just in London but in many provincial towns and cities.[4]

Terracotta contributed towards a progressive historicism in Victorian architecture. Most architects working in London accepted that their designs needed to relate, if loosely, to stylistic tradition if they were to be broadly acceptable to the public. Originality came primarily through the exploitation of the potential of ceramics for intricate modelling, curving mouldings and bold colours, and through the incorporation of narrative decoration. The arch-pragmatist Matthew Digby Wyatt was convinced that the use of relatively new and highly practical materials such as tiles, terracotta, and cast-iron was more likely to lead to novelty than 'twisting up old materials into new forms'.[5] The influence of iron on the aesthetics of Victorian architecture was restricted by an attitude that it did not constitute a proper building material, in comparison to brick and stone. The building types with the most dramatic use of iron and glass — trainsheds and exhibition halls — were likely to be regarded more as engineering than architecture. Terracotta had the advantage of being a walling material, equitable with stone, and derived from a natural raw material. It had the sanction of historical usage yet was brimming with unexploited potential for contemporary urban architecture.

Colour was accepted as an aid to originality. In the 1850s Owen Jones had put forward the principle that colour should complement style, assisting 'in the development of form' and 'light and shade'.[6] The application of this approach culminated in the bright buff, red, and pink terracottas of the 1880s and 1890s. In London terracotta was mostly worked in styles historically associated with stone, producing welcome novelty rather than a total incongruity that made a nonsense of historical precedent. The choice of colour might be dictated by the clay banks of local

factories or by questions of image and association. Bright buffs dominated in London: they presented the natural skin of a well-burnt Devon ball clay or of fireclays from the Midlands. The arch-advocate of ceramic polychromy, Halsey Ricardo, propounded a dominant rather than a secondary role for colour. He saw faience as giving architecture popular appeal, breaking through the academic irrelevance of much of London's architecture.[7] His dream was never to be realised. Most architects appreciated that bright colours appeared tawdry under the flat and often dull light characteristic of industrial cities. Colour did not, in itself, provide a meaningful architecture and the contemporary style that gave strongest potential for polychromy, Art Nouveau, gained little credence in Britain.

The Victorians were haunted by soot and the damage it wrought on their buildings. Unwilling to impose a solution through controlling pollution, they welcomed a palliative in the form of terracotta and faience. Long-established concern built up into a major crisis of confidence in the years around 1880: 'all our stone buildings have been more or less failures. The sooty particles find their way into every nook and crevice . . . all relief and contrast disappears in one dingy coating of lugubrious fur'.[8] Dingy, decaying buildings undermined civic pride, cast doubts on the benefits ascribed to industrialisation, and were associated with diseases that threatened the genteel as much as the slum dweller.

Smoke was accepted as an inevitable feature of major cities. Billowing chimneys were regarded as a sign of economic prosperity and, judging by London's nickname 'the Old Smoke', even with endearment. It was only through the sanitary reform movement that smoke eventually became associated with high mortality. Smog came to be regarded as a major threat to health at exactly the time when the revival of terracotta reached its climax. During the great fog of 1886 the mortality rate in London equalled figures for the worst years of cholera during the 1840s. Despite such damning evidence, the sanctity of *laissez-faire* outweighed pressure for reform. The most ironic instance of the triumph of narrow commercial interests is provided by the vain attempts to control two manufacturers of architectural ceramics, Doulton and Stiff of Lambeth, whose kilns belched 'noxious vapours' over Lambeth Palace and Westminster. Even action by the Archbishop of Canterbury could not restrain the two firms from adding to the sulphurous smog that was attacking the city's stonework, and hence encouraging demand for their wares.[9] The destruction caused by soot produced desperation amongst architects. Layers of grime seemed to nullify all their efforts. Victorian self-confidence was shaken by the decay of the stonework on the most prestigious building of the age, the Houses of Parliament. Discolouration and spalling were noted as early as 1848, only eight years after rebuilding had commenced.[10]

Amidst such despondency terracotta and faience offered bright colours that could be appreciated through smog, and a durability against corrosive soot. A generation of architects sought inspiration in the brightly coloured brickwork of Lombardy. However, most terracotta façades in London became stained and engrimed within a couple of decades, since they were not periodically washed down. Faience was advertised as the ultimate architectural ceramic, that would be rinsed by every shower. The *Daily Telegraph* was unconvinced by the relative merits of tiles and faience: 'That material has its uses, and not only in bathrooms and tube stations. It is easily

Figure 1. Caryatids, St Pancras Church, London, by H. W. and W. Inwood, 1818–22 (Rossi).

cleansed, and when clean it lightens our not too lucid atmosphere. But we have no desire to live in a London built of glazed ceramics in as many colours as Joseph's coat'.[11]

The terracotta revival emerged with the establishment of Coade's Manufactory at Lambeth, London in 1769. Over the next seventy years the firm provided a wide range of neo-classical ornaments and some more innovative specially commissioned designs. Most architects used terracotta as an artificial stone, directly as a substitute for carved stonework. The most fully developed example of this approach was St Pancras Church, London, built 1818–22 through a collaboration between H. W. and W. Inwood and a modeller who had left Coade by 1814, John Rossi. The four caryatids were moulded in ceramic sections and wrapped round cast-iron cores (Fig. 1). St Pancras Church was strongly criticised by the Gothic Revivalists of the early Victorian period for the way in which terracotta had been used to imitate stone and for the application of a superficial slip to some of the material to give it a fine finish.

Coade's works closed in the late 1830s and the second quarter of the nineteenth century saw the widespread use of non-ceramic artificial stone. The brick tax clearly applied to at least some types of terracotta: interest in the material revived around 1850, just as the tax was repealed. Several new firms were established in London, John Blashfield and Mark Blanchard having purchased models and moulds from Coade. Both these firms moved out of London, to Stamford, Lincolnshire in 1858, and Bishops Waltham, Hampshire respectively in the late 1860s, to escape criticisms over pollution and to be nearer to clay reserves suitable for terracotta manufacture.[12]

Blanchard supplied the bulk of the terracotta used on the Victoria and Albert Museum. The development of the cultural complex of South Kensington, including the Royal Albert Hall and the Natural History Museum, brought a new ideology to terracotta, and new approaches to its architectural employment. From the mid-1850s the Department of Science and Art, under the aegis of Prince Albert, and the secretaryship of Henry Cole, applied the reformist zeal for improving standards of design generated by the Great Exhibition of 1851. Terracotta gained strongly moralistic overtones related to the principles of economical decoration and the furthering of popular taste. Cole and his decorative artists believed that mass-produced decoration, typically moulded into Classical or Renaissance forms, would encourage a broad acceptance of cultured values and taste, and promote a respect for the status quo.

Godfrey Sykes and his fellow artists drew inspiration from Italian Renaissance monuments. The crispness of the detailing of the Certosa di Pavia was quoted as evidence of terracotta's suitability for withstanding the effects of sulphurous soot. The use of terracotta by the Department of Science and Art emerged at its most spontaneous and inspired in the Official Residences built 1862–3, and now forming the western side of the quadrangle of the Victoria and Albert Museum. Captain Francis Fowke and Godfrey Sykes collaborated to produce a façade with a crisply defined hierarchy of materials arranged within a grid, but incorporating animated figure sculpture in the spirit of work by Alfred Stevens (Fig. 2). The formula was developed on the north side of the quadrangle, begun in 1864. The feeling of spontaneity was compromised by the introduction of other ceramic materials such as glazed majolica and mosaic and through the incorporation of images celebrating dignitaries and officers involved in the development of the Museum. The Ceramic Staircase, completed inside the Museum by 1871, marks the collapse of the ideals of free ceramic modelling. Frank Moody's work bordered on the grotesque in comparison to the work of Sykes who had died in February 1866.

The Albert Hall, built 1867–71 to designs by another army engineer H. Scott, brought a new maturity to the use of terracotta in South Kensington. Scott juxtaposed plain red brick and buff dressings, a combination that would characterise the use of terracotta well into the twentieth

Figure 2. Winged cherub in decorations of ground-floor windows, Residences, Victoria and Albert Museum, London, designed by G. Sykes, 1862–3 (Blanchard).

century. The Albert Hall is also significant within the terracotta revival, in that the 80,000 blocks were supplied not by a multitude of contracts but through one big order to a firm based on the coalfields, Gibbs and Canning of Tamworth. Scott achieved a remarkable degree of repetition in his design, to utilise fully the economies possible through repeatedly pressing decorative forms in moulds. The same square-headed window design was repeated sixty-three times round the circumference of the hall (Fig. 3). The style mixed Roman precedent with high Renaissance detailing; it marked a rejection of the historicist justification for terracotta that had been achieved through the use of an earlier Italian Renaissance on the Museum. Henceforth terracotta could be used in virtually any style, and in an idiom loosely related to the traditions of stonework; the material gained its distinctiveness

through free modelling and through being burnt to bright red or buff colours. The programme of construction was arranged so that the main walls could be completed and the roof commenced before the decorative facings were applied, to minimise the effect of any delays to the supply of terracotta. The Hall was built with large blocks, up to two feet across, another feature that was to be a characteristic of the use of architectural ceramics in subsequent decades.[13]

The uses of terracotta in commercial buildings dating to the 1860s and 1870s were very variable in their quality. The material was most likely to be incorporated as the 'small change of polychromy', in conjunction with brick, stone, and tile.[14] Messrs Hunt and Crombie's premises, built 1861–2 in Eastcheap, London, provides an early surviving example of this approach. The architects, John Young and Son, combined three colours of brickwork, dressings of Bath stone with a cornice, columns, and a series of medallions of Blanchard's terracotta.[15] A soot-resistant but decorative building material was singularly appropriate for railway station hotels. The four London termini built between 1864 and 1866 all used terracotta dressings in conjunction with brick and stone. E. M. Barry made a pragmatic but rather prosaic use of terracotta in the station hotels he designed for the West End and City stations of the South Eastern Railway: at Charing Cross dating to 1864 and Cannon Street of 1866. Barry subscribed to the outdated viewpoint that terracotta should be used 'for ornament rather than construction'. He viewed the repetition of moulded details at Charing Cross or Cannon Street not as a sign of meanness, but as an honest reflection of the scale of accommodation; a concept which he described as 'the multiplication of small parts essential to the purposes of hotel life'.[16]

The experimental spirit that pervaded the mid-Victorian use of terracotta was given its fullest rein in Dulwich College, built 1866–70. Charles Barry junior and John Marriott Blashfield explored contrasting ways of working clay, pressing it into moulds, or building up intricately

Figure 3. Royal Albert Hall, London, by H. Scott and R. Townroe, 1867–71 (Gibbs and Canning).

Figure 4. Windows, Dulwich College, by C. Barry (junior), 1866–70 (Blashfield).

detailed sculpture. Barry admitted that his aim was not to forge an entirely original expression for terracotta but to work in 'the old spirit'.[17] He managed to integrate a formal, classical plan for the College with elevations that were sufficiently romantic to accommodate a medley of memories from Lombardy (Fig. 4). Barry and Blashfield gained little credit for their efforts at non-historicist originality. The chamfered panels below the ground-floor windows were condemned for looking 'as if casts had been taken in terracotta from boiler plates ... more original than attractive'.[18]

The terracotta revival might have slipped into insignificance in the 1870s. Red and buff unglazed ware could have become used for no more than modest decorative detailing in areas where brick predominated as a building material. Abetted by a range of factors including a growing concern for the effects of pollution, one architect and, to a large degree, one of his buildings, pointed the revival towards its dramatic fruition.

The Natural History Museum, designed by Alfred Waterhouse, confirmed some of the developments heralded by the Albert Hall, such as the use of terracotta to form complete wall surfaces rather than just dressings, and the supply of material from one manufacturer, in both cases Gibbs and Canning. The Museum opened in 1881 with rapturous attention being given to Waterhouse's sculptural decoration (Fig. 5). A museum of natural history offered the perfect context for narrative ornament; terracotta foliage and figures would not just be symbolic of the contents of the

Figure 5.   Animal figures on the cornice of the west wing, Natural History
Museum, by A. Waterhouse, 1873–81 (Gibbs and Canning).

Figure 6. No. 1 Old Bond Street, London, by A. Waterhouse, 1880 (Gibbs and Canning).

building, as in the case of the Victoria and Albert Museum, but an education in themselves. The Museum demonstrated a means of combining an eclectic style and the vigorous use of terracotta that was to hold sway into the next century. A symmetrical plan was combined with a loosely Romanesque style and exquisite but instructional sculpture. To one of the leading exponents of architectural terracotta, E. Ingress Bell, it was 'a Victorian building, and no other'.[19]

The culmination of the revival followed soon after the completion of the Natural History Museum. Most terracotta architecture remained closely related to the stylistic movements of the period, as worked in the more traditional materials of brick and stone. Though the 'battle of the styles' evolved into a rather more flexible contrasting and occasionally a fusion of Gothic and Renaissance styles, it is remarkable how far it remained a significant divide between the work of different architects. Led by Waterhouse's example, the free Gothic was usually realised in small blocks of simply moulded form, while the eclectic variations on the Renaissance saw the greatest use of buff material, usually in larger pieces and with more complex modelling.

Waterhouse made an extensive use of buff terracotta for the head office of the Prudential Assurance Company in Holborn, completed in 1878, but subsequently rebuilt; and for no. 1, Old Bond Street, dating to 1880 (Fig. 6). Waterhouse's characteristic combination of hot red brick and terracotta for the Prudential was first established in the provinces, being applied to their Holborn office for a major extension completed in 1901. The King's Weigh House Chapel, built 1889–91 on the edge of Mayfair, was decorated with buff terracotta made at Burmantofts, Leeds, in accordance with the specification of this colour by the Duke of Westminster for the contemporary commercial developments on his estate (Fig. 7).

Mayfair was to gain the greatest concentration of terracotta in London. A group of architects accepted the use of buff-coloured blocks moulded in a loosely Renaissance idiom, as the 'Queen Anne' style became broadened by the inclusion of motifs and forms of composition derived from the Tudors and Stuarts and from the Renaissance of northern Europe. The conscious expression of terracotta within this stylistic range emerged simultaneously in Mayfair and Chelsea, where the Duke of Westminster and Lord Cadogan took a directing interest in the development of their London estates. In 1863 the Duke of Westminster had inspected Fowke and Sykes's work in the quadrangle of the Victoria and Albert Museum. His advocacy of terracotta culminated in the designs adopted for the rebuilding of Mount

III. East front of Dulwich College, by C. Barry (junior), 1866–70 (J. M. Blashfield)

Street from *circa* 1880. Some of the new buildings displayed a degree of subtlety, while others achieved the most dense and weighty detailing possible. For numbers 117–21 Mount Street, dating to 1886, J. T. Smith produced a design that the Duke rejected as being 'very high and too elaborate in decoration'. Accepting the revised elevation, he nevertheless described it as being 'overdone and wanting in simplicity' (Fig. 8).[20]

Ernest George produced inventive and playful detailing for a series of buildings on the Cadogan Estate. At the Royal Academy exhibition of 1886, George and Peto displayed their most richly decorated Flemish style design. The house, for T. A. de la Rue and located in Cadogan Square, incorporated intricate and lively detailing. The jesters forming caryatids were light-hearted in their modelling. *The Builder* commented that none

of the decoration had any meaning or served an architectural function but conceded that 'this is the fashion now, and the authors cater for it better than most of their contemporaries'.[21]

T. E. Collcutt proved to be the only match for George in working the brick and terracotta Renaissance style in London. His first use of terracotta appears to have been for the sanitary engineer, George Jennings. Jennings was both a property developer and a clayworker, so it was natural that his works in Poole, Dorset supplied the panels of decorative strapwork, masks, and cornucopias that were set into a group of houses that he built, around 1897, in Nightingale Lane, Clapham to designs by Collcutt. Having established a close working collaboration with Doulton and in particular the decorative artist, Walter Smith, many of Collcutt's subsequent designs in

IVa.   Animal figures on the east wing, Natural History Museum, by A. Waterhouse, 1873–81 (Gibbs and Canning).

IVb.   Prudential Assurance, Holborn, London, by A. Waterhouse, 1897–1906 (J. C. Edwards).

Figure 7. King's Weigh House Chapel, Duke Street, London, by A. Waterhouse,
1889–91 (Burmantofts).

4*

Figure 8.   117–21 Mount Street, London, by
J. Smith, 1886.

London show rich sculptural detailing in compositions of considerable polish. *The Builder* appreciated the lack of 'classic gimcracks' in their Palace Theatre, Cambridge Circus dating to 1890.[22]

By the middle of the 1890s architectural fashion was turning away from eclectic decoration and brightly coloured terracotta. In 1900 the London County Council was advised to 'put down heavily on terracotta' and permit only Portland stone on the fronts of the new buildings that would line the Aldwych, part of the grand thoroughfare planned to link Holborn with the Strand.[23] The 1890s saw a flurry of optimism concerning the potential of colour as a path towards originality. The adoption of glazed terracotta, or faience as it was typically termed, followed from the development of clay bodies and glazes and could withstand frosts. Up to the 1880s faience had been primarily used for interiors and in conjunction with decorative tiling. Doulton of Lambeth led the application of glazed finishes to building exteriors. By 1876 the firm had discovered that their stoneware pottery body was resistant to both frost and soot. Doulton's stoneware was most effective when hand painted in a rich palette, such as the powdery cream, blue, and green of the shimmering entrance of the former Royal Courts of Justice Restaurant in Fleet Street, designed by G. Cuthbert and W. Wimble in 1883.

Doulton introduced a matt glazed stoneware in 1888, a crystalline glaze creating a surface akin to Carrara marble. Carraraware initiated the long-anticipated application of faience to building façades. The arch proponent of polychromy, Halsey Ricardo, found an opportunity to realise his vision in Carraraware and glazed brick, when he gained the commission for Ernest Debenham's new home. The client shared Ricardo's tastes for glazed ceramics; his store, Debenham and Freebody in Wigmore Street, was faced with white Carraraware. The exterior of his house, 8 Addison Road, built 1905–7, was a remarkable amalgam of restrained Renaissance style and vibrant colour. A round arched arcade of pink-cream Doulton's Carraraware projected from the recessed wall surfaces of glazed brick.

Faience came to be used most widely in white or grey colours and moulded in sober Renaissance styles. Ivory Carraraware was used for the extension and refacing of the Savoy Hotel, in the Strand, to designs by T. E. Collcutt. The sculptural detailing could not be very vigorous because of restrictions imposed by the stoneware body and the glazed surface. A review of the 1904 extension admitted that the modelling demanded 'no exceptional ability or skill since a free and flowing scheme of decoration is best suited for the work'.[24]

During the Edwardian period terracotta became associated with rather more mundane building types, such as pubs and underground stations, and was typically led to the infusion of some Baroque swagger or of timidly Art Nouveau detailing into otherwise staid compositions. Variety theatres symbolise the less lofty but nevertheless worthy buildings that characterised the use of terracotta and faience. Such suburban theatres as the Hackney Empire were conceived as bridging the gulf between the improving fervour of art schools and libraries, and the indulgent atmosphere of public houses. The façade designed by Frank Matcham for the Hackney Empire, of 1901, was openly enjoyable and even humorous: it gently mocked at architectural convention while showing some respect for propriety. The arch spanning the central balcony was made daringly

Figure 9. Hackney Empire, Mare Street, London, by F. Matcham, 1901 (Hathern).

renewed appreciation of terracotta is most strongly symbolised by the restoration of the two domes for the Hackney Empire over the summer of 1988, not in glass fibre or any other substitute material but in ceramic, including a new statue, produced by the Lancashire firm of Shaws of Darwen.

NOTES

1 *The Builder* 26 (1868), 582.
2 D. J. Olsen, *The Growth of Victorian London* (Penguin, Harmondsworth, 1976); 53–79 provides an overview of the Victorians' reaction to Georgian London and the cultivation of variety and expressiveness in architecture.
3 *British Architect* 29 (1888), 243–4 (243).
4 For further information on the role of the Department of Science and Art in the terracotta revival see M. Stratton, *Science and Art Closely Combined: the Organisation of Training in the Terracotta Industry 1850–1939, Construction History* 4 (1988), 35–51.
5 *The Builder* 23 (1886), 847–8 (847).
6 O. Jones, *The Grammar of Ornament* (Day, London, 1865), 6.
7 H. Ricardo, 'The Architect's Use of Enamelled Tiles', *British Clayworker* 10 (1902), 431–7 (437).
8 *Building News* 40 (1881), 253.
9 *Building News* 20 (1871), 154.
10 M. H. Port (ed.), *The Houses of Parliament* (Yale, New Haven and London, 1976), 168.
11 Quoted in *British Clayworker* 31 (1923), xlv.
12 For further information on the influence of geology on the terracotta revival see M. J. Stratton, 'The Terracotta Industry: its Distribution, Manufacturing Processes and Products', *Industrial Archaeology Review* VIII, no. 2 (1986), 194–214.
13 For further details see H. Scott, 'On the Construction of the Albert Hall', *Trans RIBA* 2 (1871–2), 83–100.
14 H. R. Hitchcock, *Early Victorian Architecture in Britain* (Yale University Press, New Haven and London), 607.
15 *The Builder* 22 (1864), 62–3.
16 E. M. Barry, *Lectures on Architecture* (John Murray, London 1881), 171–2, 363–4.
17 C. Barry (junior), *Trans RIBA* 18 (1867–8), 259–79 (260).
18 *Building News* 16 (1869), 520–1.
19 *Magazine of Art* 4 (1881), 258–62, 463–5. Quoted in F. H. W. Sheppard (ed.), *Survey of London* 38, *The Museums Area of South Kensington* (Athlone Press, London, 1975), 213.
20 F. H. W. Sheppard (ed.), *Survey of London* 40, *The Grosvenor Estate in Mayfair*, part 2 (Athlone Press, London, 1980), 328.
21 *The Builder* 50 (1886), 847.
22 *The Builder* 56 (1889), 389.
23 The recommendation was made by William Woodward to the Society of Architects. Quoted in A. S. Gray, *Edwardian Architecture* (Duckworth, London, 1985), 80.
24 *British Clayworker* 13 (1904), xx–xxi (xxi).

wide and shallow. The dome turrets were given slit windows and were surmounted by flambeaux, consisting of crowns set on columns fit for a wedding cake (Fig. 9).

The potential of faience was worked out in cinemas, culminating in exotic designs in Chinese, and Egyptian styles. The most notable survivors are the Palace Cinema, Southall of 1929 and the Carlton, Essex Road, Islington of the following year, both designed by George Coles, and faced with material supplied by Hathern of Loughborough. The use of terracotta in London virtually collapsed with the Second World War. After decades of neglect, concerted attention is now being given to its cleaning and repair. The

STRUCTURAL CARPENTRY IN LONDON BUILDING

by DAVID YEOMANS

The Fire of London marks a number of important changes in timber structures. First the Act for the Rebuilding of London[1] saw the beginning of the London Building Regulations in the form of restrictions on the use of timber and the specification of structural sizes. Forbidding the use of exposed timber in the elevations of buildings ensured that the rebuilt city would become one of brick rather than half-timbering, and the sizes of members used in floors and roofs were clearly set out for each class of building and the location of these timbers controlled to avoid fire risks. The needs of rebuilding had created an unprecedented demand for timber which could not be satisfied by native oak, the traditional building timber in this country, so that the second major change was that imported softwood began to be used in large quantities.

There were also several major building projects in and around London in the decades following, not all associated with the Fire. The completion of the rebuilding of St Paul's Cathedral was immediately followed by the building of the Queen Anne Churches, a major church-building campaign in what were then the London suburbs, while the Crown was building the Royal Hospitals at Chelsea and Greenwich, and the scale of these operations encouraged a change in the structure of the building industry. Works of this kind needed large contracting firms with sufficient capital to cope with such major undertakings because, at a time when payment for work was notoriously slow, the tradesmen would be funding the work initially.[2] Besides all these changes, the end of the seventeenth century also saw the beginning of the general use of trussed roofs. It was not the first time that these roofs were used in buildings but they were now being used in larger numbers and the conditions of rebuilding were to lead to the more rapid spread of the new structural ideas that they involved.

Thus while the first two of these changes were a direct consequence of the Fire, the development of trussed roof structures and the growth of contracting firms, although not directly related to this event, were stimulated by it. Here, however, we are concerned with the materials used, and I shall consider these by asking four simple questions. What was it that the carpenter did? And what form did the permanent structure of the building take? The answers to these will provide a background to the third question, what materials were used? And, in so far as it affected their choice, what did they cost?

At one time there was a clear distinction between the work of the joiner and that of the carpenter. Put at its simplest the carpenter did the rough work; he provided the structure of the building, the floors, partitions and roof, provided the scaffolding for the various tradesmen and built the falsework for the plasterers, bricklayers, and masons. The joiner, in contrast, did the finishing work. Whether or not the guilds had been able to enforce this distinction up to the time of the Fire, after it there was a general relaxation of their control over the trades as a way of dealing with the shortage of tradesmen in the City. There was still a distinction between the work carried out by some firms but there are bills for work by others which clearly show that some men were doing both classes of work.

Because he was providing falsework and scaffolding as well as the timber of the structure, the carpenter was a key figure on the site and for this reason many carpenters acted as general contractors and, with their ability to manage building operations, some carpenters were also speculative builders. It is also clear from a number of contracts that the carpenter might well be designing the structure as well as building it. That would have been the common practice in earlier times, but as architects had introduced new architectural forms they had also to introduce a new kind of structure so that they could be built. It was the architects who first designed these but eventually a knowledge and understanding of the new structures spread to the carpenters and it was not long before some were adopting the role of 'consulting engineers' and designing the structures for architects who had little understanding of these issues.

The structure of a typical house of the eighteenth century comprised a brick shell within which were the timber floors and timber partitions. While there might be internal masonry walls it was more convenient to reduce these to a minimum, often leaving the external walls unbraced by intersecting walls of masonry. They were therefore too slender to stand up without the stabilising effect of the floors which were built in as the brickwork was carried up. The floor structures without boarding were referred to as 'naked flooring' in the builders' manuals of the day. The normal arrangement of floors before the Fire was to span the joists at right angles to the principal elevations, breaking the width of the span across the house with a summer beam. A drawing by Leybourn showed the typical arrangement of the day (Fig. 1). The eighteenth-century practice, however, was to arrange the girders, which carried the joists, to span in the most convenient direction, sometimes even placing them diagonally in order to avoid chimney breasts (Fig. 2).

Oak joists had been obtained by splitting timbers in half, a process of conversion that produced the broad shallow joists that we associate with early timber-framed buildings. With the change from oak to softwood, sawn rather than halved timbers were used for the joists and they were now made deep and narrow, rather than

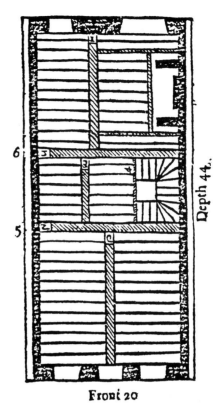

Figure 1. Late seventeenth-century floor framing from Leybourne.

shallow and broad. Two kinds of floor were used, one simply having common joists and girders while for better quality work a bridging floor was used (Fig. 2). This had binding joists at wider centres than common joists over which spanned the small bridgings, about 4″ × 5″ and about 1′ apart, which carried the boarding and which no doubt provided a stiffer floor. In good quality work there would also be separate ceiling joists.

Where the spans of floors were exceptionally long the carpenter might use trussed girders.[3] The construction of these was curious and it is not clear how the idea originated. The girder was sawn in half down the middle and the chases were cut at angles in the sawn faces to allow for the insertion of 'hard pieces of timber' (Fig. 3) which

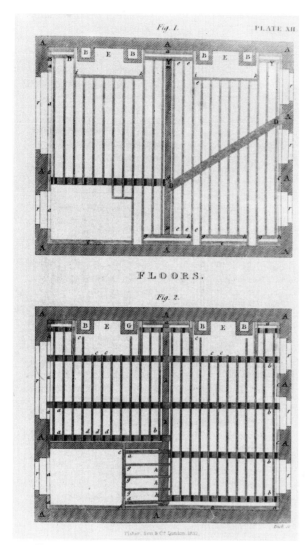

Figure 2. Typical eighteenth-century common joist floor (top) and bridging floor (bottom).

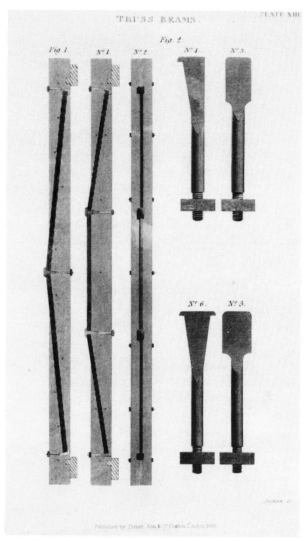

Figure 3. Arrangements for trussed beams or girders using iron bolts for tightening the trusses.

formed a kind of shallow arch within the girder. With these 'trusses' or 'trussing pieces' in place the girder was then bolted together and the trusses tightened with some form of wedge. Girders might be trussed with either two or three trussing pieces, and the wedges might be of timber or iron. The effect was to produce some precamber in the member.

Partitions were also trussed so that they would support their own weight and carry the load of floors spanning on to them (Fig. 4). The advantage of this was that the partition did not have to be carried by a wall from the floor below so that the plan of the rooms could vary on successive floors. The way that both these and the trussed girders were used in domestic construction is clearly shown in the detailed plans provided in Pain's *British Palladio*.[4] The trussed partition was, of course, a development of the trusses used for roofs. These trusses which came into common use in London buildings after the Fire, largely through the influence of Wren, facilitated a wider variety of roof forms, and much greater spans than the earlier structures.

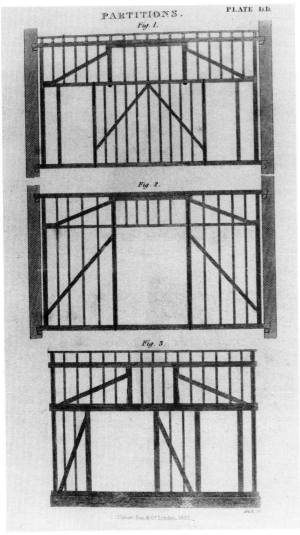

PARTITIONS.   PLATE D.D.
Fig. 1.

Fig. 2.

Fig. 3.

Figure 4. Typical trussed partitions designed to accommodate doors.

probably based on sizes that had been used in earlier forms of roof structures.

Timber was also used in masonry walls in the form of bond timbers. Batty Langley[6] described how these should be used and recommended that:

In those places on which the ends of the girders are to rest . . . lintels or bearing pieces . . . will communicate the weight equally on the whole wall. When lintels of such lengths are so laid and contain 4, 5, 6 or 7 inches in thickness, according to the thickness of the walls, they are very great strengthenings, and tie those parts very firmly together, wherefore they are called bond timbers; but lest bond timbers be not perfectly understood, I must also observe that bond timber is to be laid in walls wherein no girders are, as in end walls, cross walls &c. and which being laid throughout such walls, at every 6 or 7 ft in height and being dovetailed or cogg'd together at every outward angle of the building . . . will most firmly bind the whole together, so that, even if a foundation be unfirm, they will oblige the settlement to be regular and prevent cracks and fractures...

Certainly such timbers would act to mitigate the effects of differential settlement in the walls, but if decayed they would be worse than useless. Batty Langley does not say what kind of timber should be used for this purpose but in such a position they would be vulnerable to decay and should have been of oak heartwood, the sapwood being non-durable. But I suspect they were most often of softwood. These timbers continued to be used into the nineteenth century when designers began to recognise the problems caused by their decay and the practice was dropped. Not unnaturally the need to replace decayed bond timbers causes problems in the renovation of eighteenth-century buildings today.

What then were the timbers to be used for all this work? If we include both joinery and carpentry then there would be a large number of timbers used, since the finished work might include a variety of species. But restricting our attention to structural timbers, the issues to be considered are the switch from oak to fir from the time of the Fire, and the choice between Baltic and American timbers toward the end of the eighteenth century and the beginning of the nineteenth.

The sizes of all these members seems to have been determined through simple trial and error. The carpenters' manuals published in the eighteenth century gave recommended sizes (Table 1), although a comparison of these shows little agreement between them. It seems likely that the sizes of timbers within floors was chosen to avoid too much spring in the floor.[5] The sizes of the members recommended for roof structures are more difficult to explain. Modern analysis shows that the sizes of members recommended for roof trusses resulted in very low stresses, and they were

Table 1:

Francis Price   *Carpenters' Companion, 1733*

Girders	SMALL BUILDINGS		LARGE BUILDINGS	
	Fir	*Oak*	*Fir*	*Oak*
16' span	8″×11″	10″×13″	9.5″×13″	12″×14″
20' span	10″×12.5″	12″×14″	12″×14″	15″×15″
24' span	12″×14″	14″×15″	13.5″×15″	18″×16″
Common joists				
6' span·	6″×3″	5″×3″	5″×3″	6″×3″
9' span	9″×3″	7.5″×3″	7.5″×3″	9″×3″
12' span	12″×3″	10″×3″	10″×3″	12″×3″
Binding joists				
6' span	4″×2.5	4″×3″	4″×3″	5″×3.5″
8' span	5″×2.25″	5.5″×3″	5.5″×3″	6.5″×3.5″
10' span	6″×3″	7″×3″	7″×3″	8″×3.5″

Until the Fire of London, oak had been the natural material for use in building in Britain. It was plentiful, it was durable, and it was strong. If it had a disadvantage, it was that it was not as easy to work as some other timbers. Advising on the building of the Queen Anne Churches, Wren recommended oak as a suitable material for the roofs on the grounds that:

it will bear some negligence: the church wardens care may be defective in speedy mending of drips; they usually whitewash the church and set up their names, but neglect to preserve the roof over their head:

He went on to say that:

Next to oak is good yellow deal, which is a timber of length, and light and makes excellent work at first; but if neglected will speedily perish.[7]

As we can see from this it was the durability of the material that continued to recommend its use even though it was relatively more costly. The preferred timbers can be seen by looking at the contract[8] for Greenwich Church (Table 2). If we assume that the very best materials would have been used in work of this kind, we can see that all the principal structural materials, particularly those that might become wetted because of any defect in the roof, are all of oak with the exception of the principal rafters. From the wording of this contract it is clear that the tie-beams in this roof were divided into three lengths. Therefore, the principal rafters were by far the longest members in the structure so that it is probable that it was the unavailability of oak of this length that dictated the use of fir. One can see from the Greenwich contract that fir was acceptable for the boarding of the roof and for the ceiling joists. The structure of the galleries was of oak even though in the dry interior of the church we know that fir would have been satisfactory. Here I assume that the reason for specifying oak was largely one of tradition, that element of irrational behaviour that one can still find in specifications today. But if this was so why should ceiling joists have been of fir? My guess here, and it can be only a guess, is that it was chosen because, being a softer material, it would have been easier than oak for nailing the plaster laths.

Even though oak may have been the preferred material, the demands of the rebuilding after the Fire would have exceeded the capacity of native supplies. Besides which, while London was burning, the Dutch were also burning the English fleet at Sheerness. Wren, in the passage quoted above, noted that the demands of the navy were affecting the availability of oak for buildings. Softwood had therefore to be imported, and it is said that the Norwegians warmed themselves at the Fire of London. At the time the wood was referred to as Norwegian fir although it was Scots Pine, *Pinus sylvestris*. Although not as durable as oak it was

Table 2:

Greenwich Church

Extract from Carpentry Contract

1. The floor at the foot of the roof according to the following scantlings viz:
   beams of oak in three lengths with planks to strengthen the joints, 14″ × 12″
   Binding joists of yellow fir about 4ft. assunder, scantling 9″ × 4″
   Firings of yellow fir scantling 4″ × 3″
   Ceiling joists of yellow fir scantling 4″ × 2″
2. The roof according to the following scantlings:-
   Principal rafters in yellow fir 12″ & 10″ - 9″ & 8″.
   King post with joggles of oak, 14″ & 12″ - 8″ & 10″.
   puncheons of oak, 14″ & 10″ - 8″ & 10″.
   Braces of oak, 8 ins square.
   Small rafters of oak, 5″ × 3″.
   purlins of oak, 10″ × 7″.
   Plates of oak, 10″ × 6″
   Templets of oak, 10″ × 3″.
3. Rough boarding for lead, sap lifted off.
4. Compas covering of oak with fir ceiling joists.
5. Gallery floors of oak as follows:
   beams 9″ square, Joists 9″ × 3″
6. Boarding ye same with deal
7. Parapet to ye gallery of oak framed with trusses ye top piece 8″ × 5″ fir

Table 3:

William Pain

Pain's British Palladio or the Builders' General Assistant 1786

	Oak plank / sq. ft	
	New	Old
2″	9*d.*	6*d.*
2½″	11*d.*	7½*d.*
3″	1*s.*/1*d.*	1*s.*/0*d.*

quite acceptable for many structural uses where the timbers were normally dry in use, for floors and partitions of houses and for the structure of the roof, providing the roof was sound and the gutters did not leak. Besides, it grows straight in long lengths and is easily worked, so it had some advantages over oak apart from its price and availablility.

The price of fir inevitably meant that it became the standard construction material, but prices include the cost of labour as well as that of the basic material, and a further advantage of softwood was that it was easier to work. Salmon[9] in 1734 gave figures which show that the basic material price of oak was about 10% higher than fir, but a comparison of his prices of building components shows a greater difference, reflecting the difference in workability of the two materials. The same effect is apparent in Pain's *British Palladio* where a figure of 12*s.* to 16*s.* for labour in laying a floor of fir becomes 14*s.* to 18*s.* if it is of oak. It is also clear from Pain that the value of oak caused it to be reused where possible because he gives prices for both new and old material (Table 3). A less obvious factor affecting the relative cost of using oak and fir was that when the latter was first introduced the relative structural performance of the two was not properly understood and carpenters' manuals recommended that larger sizes be used when building with oak (Table 1). This would naturally have increased its cost disadvantage. Of course we now realise that smaller sizes of oak could have been used since it is the stronger material but Batty Langley[10] argued that 'although oak is much stronger than fir, yet it is of greater specific gravity, it must therefore have larger scantlings for the same purpose than fir which is weaker'.

There were situations where the durability of oak, though more expensive, was still needed, and in housing this was for roof laths of plain tiled roofs (Table 4). In describing the tiling of buildings Batty Langley[11] discussed the supply and sizes of these laths and noted that while:

the laths used for plain tiling should be always made of good heart of oak . . . too often when buildings are built for sale, the covetous builder uses fir laths, as being cheaper, but are of short duration.

However, softwood was apparently acceptable for pantiles, perhaps because these tiles were more watertight, but 'good yellow deal' was recommended 'as being of greater strength and duration than white deals' although it is hard to see what could have been the basis for this belief.

Table 4:
Batty Langley
The London Prices of Bricklayers'
Materials and Works,
London 1749

Prices of roofing laths

	oak heart	deal & oak sap	pantile
Prime cost/bundle	1s. — 8d.	1s. — 0d.	1s. — 6d.
Retail price, 25% profit	2s. — 1d.	1s. — 3d.	1s. — 10½d.

Pantile laths should be cut out of good yellow deals, as being of greater strength and duration than white deals.

I have touched upon the differences between oak and fir but towards the end of the eighteenth century, users of wood were to be offered a choice of softwood supplies as North American timbers became available. Construction was only one of the uses of wood with shipbuilding another major consumer, and for a maritime nation ensuring timber supplies was naturally an important aspect of economic and defence policies. Since the navy depended upon timber and the navy was so important to a colonial power, it was essential that the supply routes were secure. Oak was the timber of hull construction but fir was needed for the decks and particularly for the masts. The latter had a limited life of about fifteen years and so were a major component of ships that required periodic replacement. Baltic and Norwegian timbers were the principal sources during the eighteenth century, coming from the ports of Dantzig, Riga, Memel, and Christiania, but the supply route through the straits between Denmark, and Norway and Sweden was clearly vulnerable. Therefore, it was in our interests to seek and encourage alternative supplies. Moreover, these strategic arguments were reinforced by an economic one because the doctrine of the time sought to balance trade between countries. The Baltic countries which supplied the timber imported little from us so that there was an imbalance in this trade and for these different reasons the goverment sought to encourage timber production in North America — principally Canada — which it did by the imposition of differential tariffs.

An import tariff can only increase the cost of a commodity and the result was to drive up the price of timber and hence the costs of those items dependent upon it. When we look at the figures it is clear that at the beginning of the nineteenth century the Napoleonic wars were a more important effect on prices (Fig. 5) and, looked at from the long-term perspective, this rise in prices rather dwarfs the effect of the differential tariffs. However, it was they that were important at the time because they affected the choice of timbers that were available. We can get a good impression of how large they were by the fact that timber importers were reported to have shipped Baltic timbers to North America so that they might be sent back and imported without the high duty, the difference more than covering the extra cost of transport. The effect of an increase in prices was that builders looked for alternative materials for the same job and at the beginning of the nineteenth century this meant encouraging a change from timber to iron for construction and an increasing use of iron in conjunction with timber.

The method of levying the duty did not affect all kinds of timber equally. It discriminated against logs and square timber so that the trade shifted in

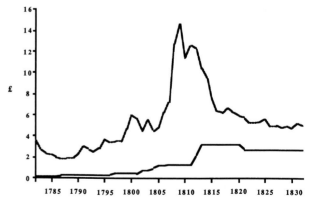

Figure 5. Prices of imported Baltic timbers (upper curve) with the duties which were imposed shown by the lower curve.

favour of the import of deals to the detriment of our sawmilling interests, but to some extent to the benefit of the user. Timber must be dried from its 'green' state before it is used in the building to avoid both decay and the effects of shrinkage that occurs during drying. If it is dried in the log, then shakes or splits tend to form as the outer part of the log dries and shrinks while the centre is still green. Cutting soon after felling helps prevent the formation of shakes, and the resulting pieces will dry all the quicker, so that timber sawn in the country of origin would almost certainly be dryer before use and freer of defects than timber imported as logs, and then sawn here. In this aspect the duties favoured the user. Unfortunately their disadvantage was that they affected the sizes that could be easily obtained because they were not based simply on the volume of timber. Flooring was ideally made of $1\frac{1}{4}$ inch deals which would be 9 inches wide. The duties on $2\frac{1}{2}$ inch deals were exactly the same as on 3 inch deals, so the former naturally became unavailable. The result was that the user had the choice of cutting the boards out of 3 inch deals, leaving $\frac{1}{2}$ inch wastage, or using battens of the right depth but only 7 inches wide. Would that we could easily obtain 7 inch boards today.

There were naturally complaints about the effect of the tariffs on the costs of building and upon the way in which they affected the availability of timber, and disquiet was such that in 1820 and 1835 there were government inquiries into these duties which explored their various effects. Our interest here is in the effect on the quality of the timbers used in building, but the enquiries also looked at their effect on shipping interests and on the development of the American Colonies which the differential duties were intended to stimulate. They are particularly interesting because they give us some insight into the practice of the day and the way that choices were made, but before looking at the evidence that was given it is worth considering the factors which affect the choice of material in a little more detail.

The 'fir' from Europe was Scots pine, *Pinus sylvestris,* known in the trade today as European redwood, and a characteristic of this timber is its variability. A modern reference work[12] says that:

The quality of the timber is affected by the conditions of growth, climate, soil, elevation etc. more than most timbers because of its wide and varying distribution and these factors affect the texture density, size and number of knots.

The effect of this was that the timbers from different regions were recognisably different and wood was bought much like we buy wine. The source of the timber was specified for its quality, whether strength or supposed durability. John White, for example, reported his own experiments to the 1835 inquiry which he said showed that the stongest timber was 'Longsound fir' from Norway. The North American timbers that became available were of different species and so naturally had different qualities. Some species were inferior in some respects to the European timber but may have been better in others; *Pinus strobus,* for example, referred to at the time as Weymouth pine, American white pine, or Quebec yellow pine, is said to be[13]

A soft weak timber, which compared to European redwood is 45% softer, 25% less resistant to shock loads, 30% weaker in bending and in compression allong the grain, and 20% less resistant to splitting and less stiff

but on the other hand:

An important characteristic of yellow pine is its low shrinkage and in this respect it is superior to all other North American softwoods except the cedars.

This quality was certainly recognised early on because James Hume told the 1835 enquiry that 'there is no such wood cut anywhere as the soft, tough yellow fir from the Colonies, for a great variety of purposes . . . such as all interior work, wainscottings, and fitting; also for case making and various things, in short, almost everything except the solid timber of buildings', and John White, an architect, regarded American timbers as good for 'a variety of purposes, in which a tender wood is necessarily useful'. Smirke reported that American yellow pine 'is more free of defective parts, from knots, and from sap; it shrinks less and it holds the glue better', and other witnesses confirmed that it generally had fewer knots than European timbers. However, a number of them disliked it because of its softness. It was unsuitable for flooring and one witness regarded it as also unsuitable for the parts of doors which might receive knocks. If Canadian yellow pine is a weak timber, this is not so of all the North American species. American red pine and Eastern Canadian spruce have similar strength properties to European redwood.

In the early nineteenth century there was a definite prejudice against the use of American timbers and the differential tariff had to overcome this as well as the higher basic price of the material. There were other properties apart from softness affecting joinery that were commented on. The tendency to warp is also important and American spruce was said to warp and so to be unsuitable for joinery. One witness referred to pitch pine (probably southern yellow pine) and regarded it as too brittle for structural use. The prejudice was mainly because the American timbers were regarded as being more susceptible to rot than the European timbers. The great fear was its lack of resistance to so-called dry rot, although this term was used at the time for almost any kind of rot. The fear was that if these susceptible North American timbers were used in connection with the supposedly more durable European timbers, the rot would take hold in the vulnerable American timbers first and then spread to the others. It was also said that dry rot might be found in these timbers on arrival in Britain and this is perhaps the clue to what was actually happening.

All the species that were used, including the European redwood, are non-durable. There was the belief at the time that resinous woods were more durable but this is not so. In fact in durable timbers it is the heartwood and not the sapwood that is resistant to decay. If the American timbers did decay more rapidly in use, it was almost certainly because fungal growth was developing during storage, or during transport. The likelihood is that either the conditions of storage in Canada or within the ships transporting the timbers, or quite probably both, were such that

the timbers remained wet enough to allow some rot to develop.

Ignorance is possibly another reason for the prejudice. In the earlier change from oak to 'fir' we can imagine that the carpenters had to adapt to the use of what was essentially an inferior material, as far as durability and strength were concerned, although it would have been easier to work for joinery and certainly cheaper. It would have taken some time before the properties of this new material were recognised, as we can see from the misunderstanding about the relative sizes to be used for structural members to which I have referred earlier. Now users were having to adjust to new species with a much greater range of properties. How quickly this was necessary can be seen from the official figures of timbers landed. Over the two years 1816–17 the quantities of deals landed in England from America was only one tenth of that imported from the Baltic countries. For the two years 1826–7 this proportion had risen to one half. When Smirke gave his evidence to the 1835 inquiry he suggested that the prejudice against American timbers might have been because it took some time for designers and builders to appreciate how they should be used properly. The same is suggested by another witness who said in evidence that:

In the work I have lately been employed on, all these sorts of (North American) deals were prohibited being used.
Prohibited by whom?
By the architects, that they should be the best Christiania deals.
The architect seems to have known there was some defect?
I do not know that; I believe it arose from custom to write Christiania in their specification.

This problem would be compounded if users could not tell the difference between the various species. One of the witnesses to the 1820 inquiry was asked if it was easy to distinguish American from European timbers. He thought that professionals would be able to tell the difference but that the various timbers were so sufficiently similar that others would not. When it was put to him that this might have led to some use of American timbers contrary to the specification, he agreed that such cheating might well have occurred. For my part I wonder if it is reasonable to assume that the professionals could always tell the difference, particularly between the different species of American timbers, when different names were being used for the same species.

In any case one needs to be aware that the Baltic timbers were not always regarded equally. George Barker, the builder of the British Museum and the National Gallery, was of the opinion that Baltic timber was also susceptible to rot and liked the red pine available from America. Armstrong thought that Dantzig and Memel firs were preferable to those from Christiania for such uses as guttering where durability was required but that they were susceptible to warping and so not suitable for joiner's work, possibly an effect of spiral growth.

An aspect of building that we still find today is an almost irrational approach to the selection of materials and the methods of working. In the absence of perfect information we rely upon rules of thumb and experience that may or may not have a satisfactory basis in fact. Experience can only be partial and of course a feature of building is that we are looking for a long-term performance and it would be difficult for designers to do this; better to stick to what you know, or at least think you know. It is reasonable to question the validity of the opinions of the witnesses to these inquiries about the behaviour of the materials. To assess the durability of a material we need to be able to monitor its performance over a number of years and in a variety of situations. Prejudice is easily developed in an atmosphere of suspicion when new materials are introduced, particularly if those new materials are more complex and require greater knowledge in their selection than those previously available. Any mistakes made in their choice, with the unfortunate results that followed, would simply have aggravated such suspicion and prejudice. It is difficult to say how much effect this prejudice had on the relative quantities of European and American timbers being used in

London. Imports of American timbers into London would have been a much smaller proportion than those suggested by the figures quoted above because Liverpool was dominated by the American trade. European timbers were simply not so readily available there where builders could not afford the same prejudice as those in London.

By 1835, however, the natural durability of timber was becoming less important. J. H. Kyan had patented his preservative treatment in 1832 and witnesses to the 1835 inquiry were already regarding it favourably. Smirke reported on the tests that he had carried out to assess its efficacy. Burnett's patent of 1838 which used chloride of zinc was a later successful alternative. At the same time there was a greater understanding of the strength properties of the different materials. Barlow's[14] work on the strength of timbers was first published in 1817, and much of his material was then incorporated into Tredgold's[15] work on carpentry, so that the nineteenth century was to see a move away from the simple reliance on a craft understanding of the behaviour of the natural material to a more scientific approach essential for its use in engineering structures.

NOTES

[1] 18–19 Chas. II, 8.

[2] Douglas Knoop and G. P. Jones, *The London Mason in the Seventeenth Century* (Manchester, 1935) have shown the way in which masons were affected by this, but the same will be true of carpenters.

[3] For a detailed account of these see Malcolm Dawes and D. T. Yeomans, 'The Timber Trussed Girder', *The Structural Engineer* 63A, No. 5 (May 1985), 147–54.

[4] William and James Pain, *British Palladio or the Builder's General Assistant* (London, 1786).

[5] David Yeomans, 'Designing the Beam, from Rules of Thumb to Calculations', *Journal of the Institute of Wood Science* 11, No. 1 (June 1987), 43–9.

[6] Batty Langley, *Ancient Masonry* (London, 1736), 353.

[7] *Wren Society* IX, 16. *Parentalia*, 318–21. Written on the setting up of the Commission for the Queen Anne Churches and therefore either 1710 or 1711.

[8] Lambeth Palace Library MS 2690/70.

[9] William Salmon, *Palladio Londonensis, or the London Art of Building* (London, 1734).

[10] Batty Langley, *Ancient Masonry*.

[11] Batty Langley, *London Prices of Bricklayers' Materials* (London, 1749), 50–71.

[12] The Timber Research and Development Association, *Timbers of the World* 2 (Construction Press, Lancaster, 1980), 134.

[13] *Ibid.*

[14] Peter Barlow, *Essay on the Strength of Timber* (London, 1817).

[15] Thomas Tredgold, *Elementary Principles of Carpentry* (London, 1820).

THE INTRODUCTION OF IRON
INTO TRADITIONAL BUILDING

by R. J. M. SUTHERLAND

In order to make the scope of this study clearer it may be helpful to define the word 'iron' and also what in the present context is a 'traditional building'.

IRON

Here 'iron' means either cast iron or wrought iron, but not steel. The properties of the two types of iron are very different, yet there is widespread confusion over this even amongst engineers.

Cast iron contains 3–4% carbon and is formed into its final shape as a liquid which is poured into a mould and solidifies. It has a granular structure, like chalk or lump sugar, and is very strong in compression but relatively weak in tension or when subjected to bending as in beams. Although available from the time of the introduction of the blast furnace around 1500, the heyday of cast iron in building was roughly in the period from 1780 to 1850 during which production increased steadily.

Wrought iron contains virtually no carbon and is formed into the required shape by hammering or rolling when it is in a pasty but never molten state. Its texture is stringy or fibrous, like timber, although this is hardly noticeable except when the material is fractured or when the surface is heavily rusted. Wrought iron is strong in tension as well as in compression and thus preferable to cast iron for beams. Nevertheless it lacks the capacity for almost effortless formation into complex shapes which is so much a feature of cast iron.

The use of wrought iron can be divided into two periods. First, the period before the introduction of cast iron, when it was very much a craft material, worked by blacksmiths on a small scale, and next the period when, following the processes perfected by Henry Cort in the 1780s, it could be produced on an increasingly industrialised basis. It became the dominant structural material in the late 1840s progressively replacing cast iron and held the field for about fifty years until it was gradually supplanted by steel towards the end of the century.

TRADITIONAL BUILDING

In this paper a 'traditional building' is taken as one which broadly looks as if it is made of simple stone or brick walls with timber floors and roof, and where any iron is subsidiary or, even if dominant, is largely hidden. Thus not only are houses 'traditional' but so are shops, clubs, hotels, public buildings, and churches, but not railway train sheds, exhibition buildings, conservatories, or factories where the iron is very much in evidence.

USES OF IRON IN THE SEVENTEENTH CENTURY

At the beginning of our period, in the late seventeenth century, iron was still mostly wrought and worked on a craft basis by blacksmiths. It was used largely for connection or for restriction. For instance in nails, screws, cramps, chains, and tie-rods, it was used for connection and in railings, gates, balcony fronts, locks, bolts, hinges, and again to some extent in chains it was used to restrict movement or to protect people or property. At that time cast iron was rare, except for cannons, firebacks, cooking pots and similar domestic articles. In most of these early applications of wrought iron considerable care was taken to make the objects elegant. Frequently they were highly decorated as in the case of Jean Tijou's superb gates within St Paul's Cathedral (Pl. **Va.**) and those at Hampton Court.

There was virtually no truly structural wrought iron in the seventeenth century. Wren's chain around the dome of St Paul's is perhaps one of few real exceptions, but otherwise small connecting plates for timber trusses were about the largest iron components.

USES OF IRON IN THE EARLY EIGHTEENTH CENTURY

In the eighteenth century the same uses of wrought iron continued but cast iron also entered the building scene, first probably for railings such as those outside St Paul's, which are said to date from 1714 although the railings have been moved so much that it is not certain whether the present ones are as old as that or not.

One early difficulty with cast iron was that it could not be produced in bulk cheaply when smelted with charcoal because the charcoal tended to crush under the total weight of the material in the blast furnace and thus the size of furnace and the total charge had to be limited. Early attempts to use coke in place of charcoal had not been successful but by 1708 Abraham Darby I had overcome these problems although there was quite a long gap between what had become possible and what was being done commercially.

CAST IRON IN BUILDING

The earliest major uses of cast iron in building date from the 1770s and 1780s, some seventy years after Darby's breakthrough. In parallel with the first cast-iron bridges, repetitive church decoration in cast iron was introduced mainly in the north and Midlands. Thus by the turn of the century cast-iron tracery, brackets, and even columns had become quite widespread as well as cast-iron pipes. To many people cast iron must have seemed just a cheap substitute for other materials, rather as plastic with printed wooden grain is looked on today. This may account for the comparative rarity of decorative cast iron in London before the 1820s. However its strength was appreciated and there are probably many cast-iron pillars hidden within traditional timber columns in eighteenth-century London houses which have not yet come to light, although perhaps not such startlingly slender ones as those in Tetbury Church in Gloucestershire of 1777–81.

The Doric pilasters of 1827–9 in Carlton House Terrace were among the earliest examples of architectural cast iron in London, making full use of repetition. (Pl. **Vb.**). John Nash had few inhibitions either about truth to materials or structural purity and it is perhaps not surprising that he should also have been one of the first users of cast-iron beams in 'polite' construction, although again not until the 1820s.

CAST-IRON BEAMS IN BUILDING

Cast-iron beams first became prominent not in London but in the textile mills of the Midlands in the 1790s and early 1800s although it is widely believed that the disastrous fire at Albion Mills near Blackfriars Bridge in 1791 was the trigger for the sudden change in mill construction. The main credit must go go Bage and Strutt who introduced brick jack-arches spanning between cast-iron beams, supported in turn on cast-iron columns, all as a substitute for the heavy but inflammable timber which previously had been standard. Their lead was quickly followed by others although the actual layout of the mills remained unchanged, with short spans (from just over two to about three metres), and a close-spaced grid of columns.

This construction had little relevance to fashionable London houses or to public buildings where there was a strong demand for larger open spaces, which could scarcely be satisfied with the current hierarchy of timber planks, joists, binders, and girders. In many cases the timber girders, even if 375 to 400 mm deep, tended to sag and the floors were often uncomfortably lively. One solution, or at least what was thought to be a solution, was to truss the girders within their depth as shown on Fig. 1. Tightening the nuts on the vertical bolts undoubtedly took out some of the initial sag and this led to the false impression that the floor was stiffer. It wasn't. If anything it had

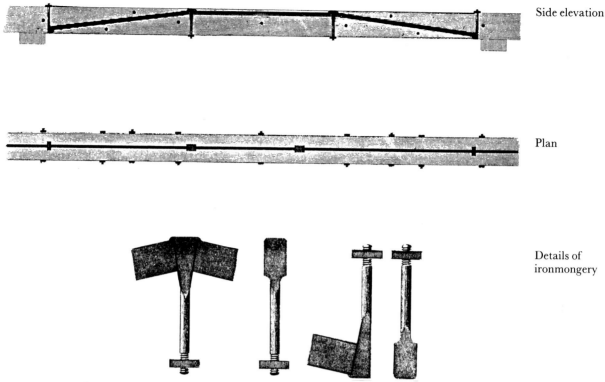

Side elevation

Plan

Details of
ironmongery

Figure 1.   Timber girder trussed with iron in its depth (hardwood struts sometimes
used for trussing instead of iron); from Nicholson's Dictionary.

become less stiff as Thomas Tredgold pointed out in 1820 in his book on carpentry[1] and as has been confirmed in a recent study.[2]

It was not until the 1820s that the answer to the problem of floor spans appeared. By that time the possible depth of cast-iron beams had become greater than that of even the largest timber girders and, although weaker in tension than in compression, cast iron was still stronger than timber, and also much stiffer. The solution was simple. All one had to do was to substitute cast-iron beams for the timber girders and continue the rest of the floor construction in timber as before.

Nash used extensive quantities of cast-iron beams in Buckingham Palace between 1826 and 1828, while Smirke used particularly large ones spanning 12.5 metres in the Kings Library of the British Museum (1824–9). Charles Barry followed with the Travellers' Club, the Reform Club, Bridgewater House and many other private and public buildings in which he made extensive

use of cast-iron beams, quite apart from the Palace of Westminster which has iron roof structures as well with a wholly original form of cast-iron roof-covering. These architects were not alone. By 1840 the cast-iron beam was firmly established.

At the Reform Club (1837–41) Barry went further than simply substituting cast iron for timber beams. Here he combined the brick jack-arches of the early iron mills with the long-span cast-iron beams of the 1820s and 1830s, thus bringing in a high level of fire resistance, good sound insulation, and floors which felt solid. In this way he gave the members of the Club generously proportioned rooms of great elegance in a building which, to the outside observer, might well be of the most traditional timber and masonry. For its time it was a technological triumph. Nevertheless there are doubts about who contributed what. Such doubts become even greater when one looks at the structure of the

Va. Wrought-iron screen by Jean Tijou in St Paul's Cathedral.

Vb. Doric pilasters of cast iron in Carlton House Terrace.

Vc. Part of elaborate cast-iron gates made by the Coalbrookdale Company for the 1851 Exhibition.

Vd. Part of same gate complex as in **Vc** after an accident showing dowelled construction.

VIa. The main staircase of Gilbert Scott's St Pancras Hotel.

VIb. Exposed riveted iron in circulation areas of St Pancras Hotel.

VIc. Exposed riveted iron in a principal bedroom of St Pancras Hotel.

VId. Robust and heavy wrought iron in railings of the nineteenth century.

VIe. Flimsy curled steel strip of constant section made in the 1980s and referred to as 'wrought iron'.

Palace of Westminster, built some ten years later and even more dependent on what would now be considered to be structural and environmental engineering.

Before pursuing the question of responsibility and credit it may be worth considering first what had happened to decorative ironwork by the middle of the nineteenth century and why the cast iron boom started to collapse around 1850.

DECORATIVE IRON IN THE NINETEENTH CENTURY

There was a clear tendency in the early nineteenth century for cast iron to take over from wrought iron for gates, railings, and balcony fronts. This was not always a complete substitution. Many designers combined the two and manufacturers became adept at riveting wrought iron, for strength, on to decorative panels of cast iron or attaching medallions, and rosettes of cast iron to delicately wrought frameworks in such a way that it was all but impossible to tell, visually, which was which.

The peak of decorative cast iron may best be exemplified by the work of the Coalbrookdale Company as shown at the 1851 Exhibition and in particular the gates designed for the Exhibition, and now re-erected in Kensington Gardens (Pl. **Vc.**). The pillars of these are of such a complexity that they could not have been cast in one piece. In practice they were assembled out of many individual castings all carefully dowelled together as has been disclosed following a recent road accident (Pl. **Vd.**).

STRUCTURAL IRON IN BUILDINGS AFTER 1850

By 1850 the brittleness of cast iron had already begun to show up, although not it seems in 'traditional' buildings. The much-publicised failures were mainly of engineering structures and, for the most part, due to identifiable causes apart from the brittle nature of the iron. For instance the Dee Bridge failure of 1847 was primarily due to a misconception in design, the progressive collapse

at Radcliffe's Mill in Oldham in 1844 seems to have been started by ill-advised remedial work while the partial collapse of the roof of the Bricklayer's Arms station was caused by a derailment. However, in each case it was the brittleness of the cast iron which made the accident serious. Cast iron tends to fail without warning.

Inevitably these and other failures like that of the Antheum at Brighton in the early 1830s contributed to a waning of confidence in cast iron. Doubtless there were structural failures of cast iron in 'traditional' buildings but probably very few. Details of any examples would be welcome.

In spite of some diminution of confidence the use of cast-iron beams in buildings would doubtless have continued (with increasing safeguards) if a rival and more reliable material had not become available. Such a material, structural wrought iron, was effectively launched largely as a result of the experimental work for the Britannia Bridge in 1845–7. Wrought-iron plates and angles could now be riveted together to form box or I Beams of almost limitless size and, what is more, beams which were not brittle and whose strength could be calculated with some precision. In addition the price gap between wrought and cast iron was narrowing so that riveted wrought-iron beams were becoming little more expensive than cast ones of equivalent capacity.

Two further factors contributed to the structural revolution of the early 1850s. One was the Metropolitan Building Act of 1844 which required staircases and access passages of public buildings to be 'fire-proof' and the other was the growing availability of wrought-iron I Beams each rolled in one piece thus reducing or even eliminating the need for riveting.

After 1850 there was almost an explosion of patented flooring systems designed for good fire-resistance and mostly incorporating wrought-iron beams rather than cast-iron ones.[3] Figs. 2 and 3 show some typical examples.

It can be seen in Fig. 2 that some of these developed from the jack-arches of the early iron mills but with concrete replacing the brick arches, and wrought instead of cast-iron beams. Some

Fairbairn. Masonry jack-arches spanning between cast-iron beams (a development from the early iron mills).

Fairbairn. Wrought-iron beams with riveted iron plate forming permanent shuttering to concrete.

Moreland. A variant on Fairbairn's system (above) using light corrugated iron shuttering.

Dennett & Ingle. Alternative concrete arch forms with wrought-iron beams and re-used shuttering.

Figure 2. Typical examples of fire-resistant floors with arched soffits.

used permanent sheet iron formers to the concrete arches and others were based on removable shuttering as in the case of the system developed by Dennett and Ingle and used for the Foreign, Home and Colonial offices and in other London buildings. In the floors of the St Pancras Hotel the wrought-iron beams are spaced farther apart (up to about 4 metres) with light wrought-iron trusses with curved tops supporting permanent corrugated sheeting on to which the concrete was cast.

One popular 'fireproof' system was the Fox & Barrett floor shown on Fig. 3. This depended on close-spaced wrought-iron joists with timber slats spanning between them. Plaster was forced between the slats as in traditional decorative plaster work and then concrete was cast on top. This system can be found today in the Albert Hall and in many other London buildings.

The simple filler joint floor (also shown on Fig. 3), which could be said to have developed from the Fox & Barrett type, was one of the most widely used in the late nineteenth and early twentieth centuries but now supplanted by reinforced concrete.

From the 1890s onwards steel gradually took over from wrought iron for structural sections while the imported reinforced concrete systems developed here in the same period. However these are outside the scope of this study.

It can be seen that the dominant period of structural cast iron in London's buildings was from about 1820 to 1850, although cast-iron columns were still used until well into the present century. Wrought iron, rolled and riveted, was the most broadly favoured material for virtually the whole second half of the nineteenth century.

Although there are quite extensive records of the use of iron in buildings in the nineteenth century and many examples still survive, there are two areas where information is still sparse and which merit discussion. These are:

(a)   Who detailed the ironwork in buildings in each period?

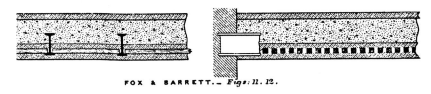

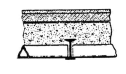

FOX & BARRETT._ *Figs: 11. 12.*

Fox & Barrett floor. Timber slats encased in plaster spanning between small wrought-iron beams with concrete topping.

LIVERPOOL "FLAGS"._ *Figs: 13. 14.*

Liverpool flags. A variant on the Fox & Barrett floor using ceramic tiles of triangular section in place of timber.

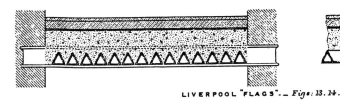

DOULTON - PETO._ *Fig: 47.*

Doulton – Peto. One of many flooring systems with lightweight ceramic blocks spanning between wrought-iron beams (beam soffits also protected from fire).

Filler joist flooring. Wrought-iron beams fully encased in concrete. Very popular in late nineteenth and early twentieth centuries.

Figure 3. Typical examples of fire-resistant floors with flat soffits.

(b) What was the attitude of the architectural profession and its patrons to the appearance of iron?

WHO DETAILED THE STRUCTURAL IRONWORK IN BUILDINGS?

This question is most easily answered for the period after 1850 although even here much depends on informed conjecture rather than surviving records. Nevertheless it does seem clear that the manufacturers of the flooring systems provided a design service for architects in the same way that specialist manufacturers make drawings today. The architect defined the layout, the wall thicknesses, all finishes, and waterproofing details. He was responsible for the overall stability of the building (no real problem at that time) but only needed to make sure that the proprietary flooring details fitted in with everything else. This may explain why the surviving architectural drawings of this period show so few structural details, of floors in particular.

It is in the period up to 1850 that there are the greatest doubts. There were text books on carpentry in the eighteenth and early nineteenth centuries which architects could have used as guides and from the early 1820s there were books and papers on cast iron, notably by Thomas Tredgold from 1822[4] and by Eaton Hodgkinson in the 1830s, and 1840s.[5]

The shapes of the cast-iron beams used give some indication of the sources of the thinking. Tredgold, although reliable on timber, went very wrong on cast-iron beams, deducing from some

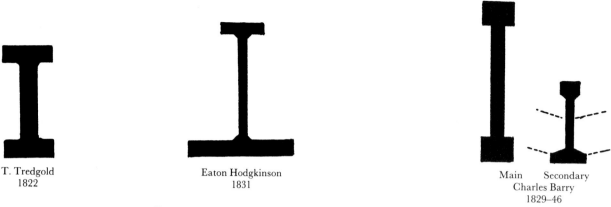

T. Tredgold
1822

Eaton Hodgkinson
1831

Main   Secondary
Charles Barry
1829–46

Figure 4.   Comparative cross-sections of cast-iron beams.

small-scale tests that the material was equally strong in tension, compression, and bending. He thus advocated beams of a symmetrical I section but with permissible loads which in some cases were virtually breaking loads.[6] Eaton Hodgkinson showed by experiment that cast iron was about a sixth as strong in tension as in compression and published his 'ideal section' with a greatly enlarged tensile flange in 1831 (Fig. 4); he also developed a generally reliable theory to go with it. In spite of this Tredgold's book went on into new editions up to 1865, admittedly with Eaton Hodgkinson's work bound in from 1842 but with no direct refutation of Tredgold's error.

Did the architects read and use these books or did they rely on the iron-founders, and did the iron-founders in turn rely on these books and, if so, on which? One wonders whether some of the larger firms of architects had 'in-house' experts to sort out the technology, or whether they consulted individual engineers.

Proof testing certainly played a large part in the approval of cast-iron beams but few records remain and it is not certain either how widespread this testing was or exactly what the test loads were or represented.

It is because of all these doubts that the drawings by Charles Barry in the RIBA collection are both so valuable and so frustrating, as are those of the Palace of Westminster in the Public Record Office. Barry's drawings in the RIBA show very precise beam dimensions and they also

show proof-loads to be applied with expected deflections. Some of the drawings, of the Reform Club in particular, have actual test loads added in a different hand below the figures demanded. Many of these drawings are signed by Barry and cover more than just the cast-iron members; they appear to be part of the general architectural set for the particular building to which the cast-iron details, possibly prepared by others, have been added.

The drawings of the ironwork for the Palace of Westminster give similar details of size, proof-load and deflection but are not signed, and in this case appear to be a completely separate set, which may well have been prepared by the contractor for the ironwork.

The main iron beams found so far on Barry's drawings or in actual buildings by him, are virtually all of the symmetrical I section, or 'Tredgold' type, and for the most part only the small binders have slightly broader bottom flanges, where these are needed to support jack-arches (Fig. 4). This is so in the Palace of Westminster and in 12 Kensington Palace Gardens, both dating from the mid-1840s — well after Eaton Hodgkinson's discoveries — as well as in the earlier Reform and Travellers' Clubs. Further, many of the proof-loads are very high compared with strengths one would expect from simple theoretical analysis.

These findings point to Barry, or whoever designed the cast iron, working to Tredgold's erroneous theory and continuing to use it well after it had been shown to be wrong. This is still very much a first conclusion based on spot checks which have also disclosed some inconsistencies. The search for further evidence on Barry's method of working must continue. I hasten to say that nothing found here casts any doubt on the adequacy of the beams in the buildings. If they passed these proof-loads their quality could hardly be in doubt.

It would be very useful if equivalent caches of ironwork drawings for buildings designed by other architects of the period could be found. Smirke's big beams of the 1820s for the British Museum were designed and tested by Rastrick, one of the major engineers of the time, who was then also the manufacturer. Rastrick illustrated the test method for these in his evidence to the Royal Commission on the Application of Iron to Railway Structures of 1849 but, maddeningly, he did not state the loads applied, and said nothing on the strengths expected.

Any leads to further information would be welcome.

ATTITUDES OF THE ARCHITECTURAL PROFESSION AND THEIR PATRONS TO THE APPEARANCE OF IRON

If there are still major doubts on who prepared the details of structural ironwork for buildings in the first half of the nineteenth century, there are even greater doubts on architectural attitudes to it throughout the century. Should it always be hidden or, in the extreme, was its use decent or even moral?

Surprisingly little appears to have been said or written on the subject. While the slenderness of iron structures might have been welcomed in buildings like the Palm House at Kew and tolerated in railway stations, there is little evidence of any enthusiasm to expose the material to view in more traditional buildings, in London anyway.

Iron beams were useful, like drains, and it seems that, like drains, they were expected to perform their function without drawing attention to themselves. The great civil engineering works of the century such as the Britannia Bridge or Box Tunnel might be worthy of debate but when it came to the new Foreign or Colonial offices it seems that few wished to know what the floors were made of. These and similar floors were hardly on the heroic scale of the civil engineering achievements.

Although in the nineteenth century most architects preferred to keep their iron structures unseen and unmentioned there were some advocates of a new iron architecture, notably William Vose Pickett, who wrote a book in 1845 called 'New System of Architecture founded on the forms of Nature and Developing the Properties of Metals'. He wrote with the crusading zeal of some of the later pioneers of the modern movement but seemed to have had little understanding of the problems of construction.

In 1880 James Picton presented a paper to the RIBA with the title 'Iron as a Material for Architectural Construction'. This was another piece of campaigning, in which he urged architects to apply their genius to iron, but it received only a limited response in the ensuing discussion. G. E. Street came out of this discussion best but hardly in favour of iron. Starting with 'to tell the truth the subject of this evening has no great attractions for me', he attacked Gilbert Scott's Albert Memorial as a visual sham which could not work without its iron box girders and also attacked all the buildings which seemed to rest on sheets of plate glass, going on to say of engineers 'in proportion as their art has become more scientific it has become less beautiful'. He believed in planning rather than iron beams to solve his layout problems and castigated the Americans for the iron houses in New York which were merely 'bad imitations of stone'. The one form of building in iron which he singled out for some praise was the 'public street retiring places' which he saw as a better model than any other 'if we are to build houses of iron'.

I have failed to find any equivalent statement by Gilbert Scott. He is generally seen as one who used iron liberally but neither expressed it nor described it. Nevertheless there are apparent inconsistencies in his practice. In the St Pancras Hotel he designed a magnificent main staircase in iron all covered decoratively as shown in Pl. **VIa.**, yet in public circulation spaces and in what must have been the best bedrooms of the hotel he left parts of the rivet-studded ironwork exposed in its stark simplicity (Pl. **VIb.** and **c.**). One cannot help wondering why. There are no signs of encasement having been removed.[7]

CONCLUSIONS

The introduction of structural iron into traditional building in London (and elsewhere) can only be seen as a success story. The techniques became progressively better and by the late nineteenth century it was structural iron rather than decorative or 'restrictive' iron which was most in demand. Nevertheless, magnificent gates and railings were still being made both in wrought and cast iron.

Today structural wrought iron has been displaced entirely by structural steel and no wrought iron is being made in Britain. This is sad because steel lacks the malleable quality of wrought iron and one only needs to compare the flowing shapes of wrought iron in Pl. **VId.** with today's curled strip of constant section as shown in Pl. **VIe.** to appreciate the decline in quality since the nineteenth century. Likewise today cast iron, although revived to some extent in the last year or two, lacks the robustness and magnificence of its nineteenth-century equivalent.

BIBLIOGRAPHY

1. Gloag, John and Bridgewater, Derek, *A history of cast iron in architecture* (George Allen & Unwin, London, 1948)

2. Singer, Charles *et al.* (Ed.), *A history of technology*, Oxford, IV, *c.* 1750–*c.* 1850; Hamilton, S.B. *Building and civil engineering construction*, 442–88. V, *c.* 1850–*c.* 1900, Hamilton, S.B. *Building materials and techniques*, 466–98.

3. Webster, John J., *Fire-proof construction*, Min. Proc. I.C.E., Vol. CV (1892) 249–88.

4. Hamilton, S. B., *A short history of structural fire protection of buildings particularly in England;* National Building Studies No. 27 (HMSO 1958).

5. Charles E. Peterson (Ed.), *Building Early America* (Chilton Book Co. Radnor, Penn. USA, 1976). Chapter by Sutherland, R.J.M. 'Pioneer British contributions to structural iron and concrete 1770–1855'.

6. Sutherland, R.J.M., *Thomas Tredgold (1788–1829): Some aspects of his work Part 3: Cast iron*, Trans. Newcomen Society, 51 (1979–80), 71–82.

7. Port M. H. (Ed.), *The Houses of Parliament* (Yale University Press, 1976). Chapter by Dr Denis Smith, 'The Techniques of Building'.

SIGNIFICANT BUILDINGS IN RELATION TO THE INTRODUCTION OF IRON INTO TRADITIONAL BUILDING SINCE THE GREAT FIRE

1. St Paul's Cathedral stands out for early structural iron (chain around dome), for early cast-iron railings and above all for Jean Tijou's superb wrought iron (late seventeenth and early eighteenth century).

2. For the introduction of cast-iron flooring the works of Nash, Smirke, and Barry are notable, particularly Barry's Reform Club. However virtually none of this is visible (1820s and 1830s).

3. Charles Barry's Palace of Westminster represents the peak of structural cast iron and the early combination of this with wrought iron (in the roof) together with decorative cast iron and cast-iron roof cladding (1840s).

4. For fire-resistant floors generally after 1850, with wrought-iron beams, Gilbert Scott's Foreign, Home and Colonial Offices, St Pancras Hotel, Grosvenor Hotel, Victoria, the Albert Hall, Covent Garden Opera House, and the Natural History Museum are just typical examples. In very few cases are there any external signs of the use of iron.

5. The gates and railings by the Coalbrookdale Company for the Great Exhibition Building (1851), now re-erected in Kensington Gardens, probably show the climax in developing cast iron as a decorative material.

NOTES

[1] Thomas Tredgold, *Elementary Principles of Carpentry* (London, 1820).

[2] M. H. Dawes and D. T. Yeomans, 'The timber trussed girder', The Structural Engineer 63A, No. 5 (May 1985).

[3] See bibliography item 3.

[4] Thomas Tredgold, *A practical essay on the strength of cast iron* (J. Taylor, London, 1822).

[5] Eaton Hodgkinson, *Theoretical and experimental researches to ascertain the strength and best forms of iron beams*, Memoirs Literary and Philosophical Society of Manchester, 2nd Series, V (London, 1831). Republished with further information as a second part to the 4th Edition of item 4 above (1842).

[6] See bibliography item 6. Also paper *Recognition and appraisal of ferrous metals* for symposium at Bath University 10–12 July 1985, *Building Appraisal, Maintenance and Preservation.*

[7] Peter Guillery has since pointed out that similarly exposed rivets were found recently in the Langham Hotel, again dating from the 1860s.

MECHANISATION AND STANDARDISATION
Some Services and Finishings in the Victorian House

by IAN GRANT

The nineteenth century differed considerably from previous ones in that, into the already sophisticated process of building, was added the requirement of incorporating a range of hitherto unknown technology. Gas lighting, multiple drainage, heating systems, internal communications (bells and speaking tubes), all had to be absorbed into the still largely traditional building process.

Building techniques themselves varied surprisingly little in domestic work right up until the end of the century, and metal, glass or reinforced concrete barely appeared before the beginning of the twentieth century, except in industrial buildings and engineering works.

Much nineteenth-century service technology would seem to us to have been treated extemely casually; we find water supply pipes and drainage inaccessibly built into the structure until the very end of the period under review, and lead gas pipes snaked about within walls and behind the plaster, whilst under the floors, gasolier vents ran from central ceiling roses to external airbricks with no provision for their maintenance. Most houses also contained a cats' cradle of bell wires, with their direction cranks, tin guide tubes, and tension springs. This hidden and even dangerous world merits at least a brief examination.

The immensely expanded building programme during the nineteenth century seems to have led to the adoption of an even greater amount of standardisation than had been the practice hitherto in the finishing trades. The universally popular four-panel door for instance (its smallest usual size being 2′8″ × 6′8″) was produced in extending 2″ increments of sizes almost 'ad infinitum'. The standard marble fire-surround was made in

modules of 6″ in length, and the furniture industry similarly standardised the mandatory overmantel glass to fit it. This trend seems also to deserve a glance.

GAS LIGHTING

Gas lighting was first introduced into London in 1807, and by the mid-1820s there were 40,000 gas lamps over 215 miles of street, irrespective of the outlets within buildings.

Internal gas systems were run in a fashion that would seem extremely casual to present day practice, especially in view of the dangerous nature of the product. Flexible lead pipes were buried in plaster and run through floors, fittings were placed in close proximity to open fires, or near to curtains, and bed hangings; indeed gas explosions were not uncommon, and in the average terrace house the effect was to blow out the front!

Until the invention of the incandescent mantle in the mid-1880s (only really as a counter to the increasing threat from electric lighting) little progress had been made in raising the light level of the naked gas flames except by increasing their number, with a consequent rise in internal atmospheric temperature. The 'vitiated air' that so obsessed the Victorians would seem to have been not so much polluted as hot, combined with the odours of a public that was still inadequately provided with the easy means of personal hygiene.

WATER SUPPLY AND DRAINAGE

Most houses, certainly in London, were provided with drainage connections by the beginning of the nineteenth century, and with piped water, but the head to raise this above basement level varied greatly, especially as most of the water was supplied by small private companies with slender financial resources for improvements.

Until the wholesale replacement of wooden water mains with cast iron, which only got under way in the late 1840s, the question of head was purely academic. The custom of washing in water (hot or cold!) that had been carried up by servants from the basement persisted until almost the end of the century, and the provision of bathrooms in new houses had barely begun by the 1850s.

The continuously popular archetypal Victorian water closet, the 'valve closet', had in fact been developed in the eighteenth century, and perfected by Bramah, who took out a patent in 1778.

Despite the invention of the simple and cheap 'wash-out' closet by Twyford in the early 1870s, the valve closet with its expensive and complicated machinery remained firmly in favour throughout the nineteenth century, and even as late as 1893 George Reid stated in 'Practical Sanitation' that 'the Valve Closet is undoubtedly the best, provided that economy is not considered'!

Towards the end of the nineteenth century we find that catalogues of sanitary ware offered both types of closet on the same page.

INTERNAL COMMUNICATIONS

The problem of internal communications, especially for summoning servants, continually exercised Victorian ingenuity, but until the advent of electric bells and telephones it was one that was almost beyond the reach of available technology.

The only satisfactory system, which was installed in every new house but the most humble, was the mechanical bell, which had been common since the late eighteenth century. It consisted in a lever or pull (sometimes several) in every room, which, when operated, exerted a tension over a copper wire, and eventually jerked the spring of a bell situated in the servants' quarters. Since these areas might be a considerable distance from the source of the call, the bell-hangers needed consid-

erable expertise to correctly adjust the system through changes in horizontal and vertical direction in order to maintain the required mechanical force. Houses were penetrated by a web of bell wires (slipping loosely through tin tubes and running under floors), which were guided by pivoted direction cranks and braced by springs. The bronze bells, identified by labels and different tones, were lined up outside the service areas and in the servants' bedrooms.

Speaking tubes, although known about very early in the nineteenth century, do not seem to have come into common usage until the last third, and they only functioned satisfactorily over short distances, and best if the tube were kept straight. They became popular as a means of communication between dining room and kitchen, and were provided at each end with a conical mouthpiece into which a whistle was plugged. The call was first given by removing the whistle and blowing into the mouthpiece, thereby sounding the whistle at the opposite end. The person thus called would then remove the whistle and listen to the shouted message.

All these items of technology were expected to be absorbed invisibly into the traditional structure.

STANDARDISATION

With so many new demands to be accommodated, it is hardly surprising that the nineteenth-century building industry was happy to accept an even greater degree of standardisation than had previously been available.

The universal nineteenth-century marble fire surround, constructed of cheap marble offcuts of between 1″ to 2″ thick, tended to be enriched by reeding on the jambs and head, with 'bulls-eye' corners until around 1850. The fashion then developed for all surface ornament to be omitted, but for two massive and sometimes crudely carved brackets to be provided at either end of the mantel shelf. Towards the end of the century, increasing taste for small-scale enrichment was met by such products as enamelled slate, where a painted

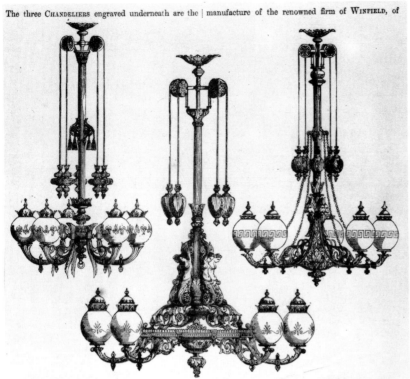

The three CHANDELIERS engraved underneath are the | manufacture of the renowned firm of WINFIELD, of

Birmingham; they are of bronze, gilt, and exhibit considerable taste and skill in design, while the workmanship is of the highest order of merit. Few foreigners surpass the British manufacturer in brilliancy of metal.

Figure 1. Water slide gasoliers — from the illustrated catalogue of the International Exhibition, London, 1862.

Nº 3106. DIAR 34 IN.

Figure 2. Perforated ceiling rose — from the catalogue of the Papier Mâché Company, London, 1874.

No. 48. IMPROVED PATENT SELF-HEATING GAS BATH.
With Linen Warmer and Atmospheric Burner.

(Registered as an Article of Utility.)

Consuming only half the amount of Gas used by the ordinary Ring Burner, causing neither Smoke nor Smell, nor the Deposit
of Soot, so objectionable in the old principle.

With **Massive Semi-Roman Bead to Bath,** Japanned Green Marble outside and White inside,
With **Town-made Taps and Brass Levers for Cold and Waste** ...   ... Price, 5 feet   £15   15   0
                                                                                                                5 feet 6 inches   16   16   0
                                  If without Levers and Taps, less £2 5 0

If Bath made with **Round Ends** same price, and if with ordinary Ring Burner, 15s. less

Figure 3.   Gas Bath — from the catalogue of Tin, Iron-Plate, and Japanned Wares by B. Perkins &
Son, London, 1897.

simulation of coloured marble inlays was baked onto slate slabs of the same basic form as had been popular for eighty years. The shapes and sizes remained remarkably consistent, and marble masons turned them out in a series of increases to fit the humblest to the grandest apartments. The length of the mantel shelf extended in 6″ increments, with the width of the jambs and head expanding in proportion. Steam cutting and carving machinery was universal by the middle of the century, and large builders like Cubitt operated a veritable production line. Similar standardisation is noticeable in joinery pro-

duction, with the more elaborate mouldings being made up out of a series of pre-cut profiles rather than being made individually. I have already mentioned the ubiquitous nineteenth-century four-panel door. The smallest universally used size was 2′ 8″ × 6′ 8″, and it is to be found in rising 2″ increments up to 7′ 6″ or 8′ 0″. The only difference that is apparent is that, although the stiles and rails always seem to maintain a standard full width of 4″ (except in very large doors when they can be found up to 5½″), the lock and bottom rails in early nineteenth-century examples are sometimes as much as 11″ in depth, whereas in

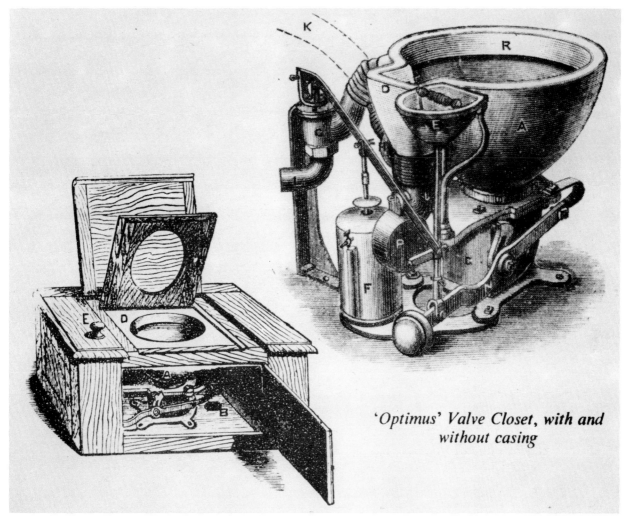

Figure 4. 'Optimus' valve closet, with and without casing — illustration from 'Clean and Decent', London, 1960.

the last half of the century they seem to have gradually been reduced to as little as 7½". It appears also that in the first half of the century the lock rail was placed very low; after 1850 the lock rail tended to be gradually raised towards the centre of the door, giving a very different appearance to early or late nineteenth-century doors, although the basic four-panel form continued to be by far the most common.

BIBLIOGRAPHY

Webster and Parkes, *Encyclopaedia of Domestic Economy* (London, 1844).

Hellyer, S S., *The Plumber and Sanitary Houses* (London, 1877).

Reid, George, *Practical Sanitation* (London, 1892).

O'Dea, W. T., *Lighting* 1 and 2 (London H.M.S.O., 1967).

Trendall, E. W., *Exterior and Interior Finishings* (London, 1852).

SIGNIFICANT BUILDING

The Reform Club, London (which incorporates examples of almost every matter touched upon in the text).

NOTES TO ILLUSTRATIONS

Figure 1. Water slide gasoliers. The Victorians were ever inventive of ingenious devices, and the 'water slide' was intended to allow adjustment of the height of the light source and facilitate cleaning and maintenance. The usual fixed

Figure 5. Bell fittings — from the Illustrated Price List and General Guide of A. Oakden & Sons Ltd. (*c.* 1900–10).

Figure 6. Water-colour drawing of a parlour (*c.* 1850–60) showing many elements touched upon in the text.

tube was replaced by a telescopic connection, and the fixture was counterweighted by suspended weights on chains and pulleys. Gas was prevented from escaping by a water seal within the tube, which was replenished from the top. Unfortunately the heat from the burners tended to evaporate the water extremely quickly, and even the practice of pouring a little paraffin oil onto the water surface made little improvement. Gas escapes and explosions often happened, but fire-brigade officers issued warnings to little effect. Like much Victorian technology, a basically inefficient device enjoyed a surprisingly long run of popularity.

Figure 2. Perforated ceiling rose. The universal large central ceiling light fitting demanded an ornamental 'rose' to mark its position, and the advent of gas lighting required the invention of ways to dispose of the added heat and fumes. Ventilator pipes running from the ceiling centre through the floor became common practice, and papier mâché lent itself much more readily than plaster to the formation of the perforations which were required. In earlier plasterwork the perforations were relatively small, but in later examples the whole centre of the 'rose' virtually disappeared, and the void was concealed by an ornamental metal grille.

Figure 3. Improved patent self-heating gas bath. Apart from coal and wood, gas was the only heat source available to the Victorians, and even this use only developed towards the end of the century. Nineteenth-century technology made use of available power sources in ways that would be considered rather dangerous nowadays, as witness this frightening apparatus. At least in this example the water was heated in a container beside the bath, rather than by flames playing onto the bath itself, as was the practice in some other models.

Figure 4. 'Optimus' valve closet, shown with and without casing. The valve closet was invented in the eighteenth century, and patented by Bramah in 1778; it remained popular throughout the nineteenth century and into the twentieth, despite the development of the infinitely more practical 'wash-out' and 'wash-down' closets from the 1870s onwards. It was an extremely complicated piece of machinery, and it is easy to see from these pictures why it was always encased. The base of the pan was sealed by a hinged plug which was closed by a heavy counterweight, and dependent on a leather washer for holding the water seal. The supply of water was regulated by a flushing valve (from which the name derives) and this was activated by raising the handle or knob in the seat; the contents of the pan would then be carried away into a lead soil pipe, which was sometimes provided with two consecutive U-traps at its junction with the appliance.

Figure 5. Bell furniture. Until the invention of a practical electrical bell, mechanically operated bells were virtually the only means of internal communication in buildings. They were in use throughout the nineteenth century, and the bell-hanger was a highly trained and skilful tradesman. Copper wires ran through floors and in tin tubes buried in the wall plaster from the pulls in each room to a range of bells in the servants' quarters, and the difficulty of precisely tensioning the wires through their numerous changes in direction required the greatest degree of expertise.

Figure 6. A drawing room (water-colour, English *c.* 1850–60, artist unknown). Many of the devices of domestic technology mentioned above are evident in this picture. There is a standard early nineteenth-century marble 'bulls-eye' fire surround, surmounted by a gilt-framed looking-glass of equal width but later fashion; this in its turn is reflected in a console-glass on the opposite wall. Matching gilt pelmets at the windows complete the highly sophisticated 'suiting' of the fixed furniture. The plaster ceiling rose, marking the position of the central light fitting, does not seem to be perforated, but the fitting itself appears to be a rarely lit chandelier, hung mainly for its 'furnishing' effect. A tapestry bell pull may be seen hanging to the right of the fireplace, connected to the lever which is fitted near the ceiling. The set of neo-rococo or Modern French furniture and the patterned wallpaper and carpet complete a remarkably characteristic mid-century interior, the only curious feature of which is the presence of full-size copies of two of Canova's Dancing Girls!

THE BROOKING COLLECTION
Application in the Conservation Field

by CHARLES BROOKING

The Brooking Collection charts the developments of style and construction of doors, windows, ironmongery, firegrates, staircases, and rainwater-heads of the period 1660 to the present, with a strong emphasis on the eighteenth and nineteenth centuries. The purpose of this study is to provide a national resource centre for architects and others involved in restoration work, where features such as glazing-bars and door furniture can be examined in detail. The Collection comprises in the region of 25,000 items, and has been built up over the past twenty-five years personally by Charles Brooking. All the details preserved were rescued from buildings undergoing demolition or drastic alteration,and most of the major items came from London sites, which included in 1988 Liverpool Street Station (c. 1874–92), the Langham Hotel (c. 1864) and Lutyens's Britannic House, Finsbury Circus. Features are rescued from all kinds of building except churches. The detailed record offered by the Collection is vital to the correct understanding of the finer details which play an important part in building design.

Great emphasis is put on covering items hitherto unexplored, such as skirtings, architraves and the development of the sash window, wrought iron, leaded-light casement windows, and simple vernacular joinery illustrating changing designs in rural and urban areas. Alongside the complete elements is an extensive 'library' of sections — including architraves, casement-frames, sash-boxes, skirtings, and doors. This incorporates also mounted displays of glazing-bars and sash-horns for dating purposes. Joinery details are often half-stripped of their accumulated layers of paint to reveal the true profile of the mouldings, and some interesting aspects of original paint treatment have come to light.

Windows, doors, architraves, and related ironmongery c. 1660–1960 are a most vital area that has not been covered in this kind of detail by any other museum. Their evolution is comprehensively illustrated by complete examples and sections. This is one of the most important areas covered by the Collection, because it is here that some of the most serious mistakes in restoration work are made. A method of dating, developed as part of the sash-window study, is centred on the sash-pulley, and evolved as thousands of pulleys were examined. With knowledge and understanding of mouldings and joinery details, it is possible, even in the most difficult circumstances, to ascertain that a box-frame or sash-pulley has been replaced. In London, early examples had oak or boxwood pulley-wheels (unless brass was used) set directly into the pulley-styles, pivoted from one side; or a separate oak surround or case was made for the wheel, to facilitate removal (this was housed in the pulley-style). By the mid-eighteenth century, sash-pulleys of brass with wrought-iron cases were in use, and in the 1770s cast-iron pulleys were introduced. From 1780, there were many variations, and the pulley display charts the major stylistic developments. This method has often cleared up difficult dating problems, where a building has been drastically altered.

Staircases. A similar approach to that outlined above is adopted for staircases. A module of approximately 4' is used to illustrate hand-rail and baluster design, with sections of hand-rail as necessary to highlight the intricate methods of construction.

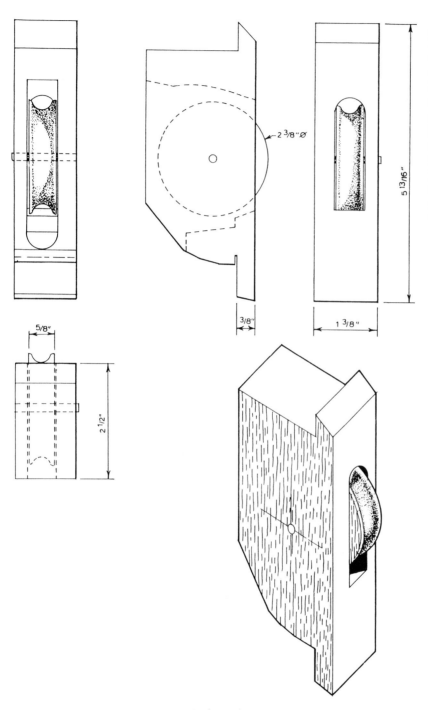

Figure 1. Two examples from the
Brooking Collection of sash-pulleys,
which numbers 5,000 different
varieties, and is a dating method for
buildings — particularly later
alterations and windows where more
obvious period details have been
lost. This is a typical early
eighteenth-century oak sash-pulley
from Bedford Row, London, built in
1718. The transition from oak to
metal, and then cast iron, has been
charted in great detail by the
Collection.

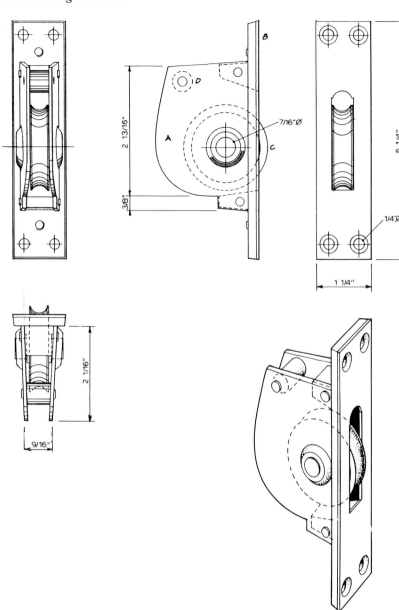

Figure 2. Cast-iron and brass axle pulley of a pattern introduced in the late eighteenth century which remained in production, with slight changes to the cast-iron sides and axle, until the mid-nineteenth century. This example, which is identical to those at the City of London Club, built in 1833, and the British Museum, comes from the 1830s Nursery Floor (designed by Nash) at Buckingham Palace. A comprehensive study is being made of the box-frame construction of sash windows and sash-pulleys, with an emphasis on their use as a dating guide.

Rainwater-Heads. No other exhibition charts the development of this important feature, from the lead varieties of the eighteenth century to the cast-iron elaborate patterns made until 1939. The transition from lead to cast-iron is crucial, and is often misunderstood by architects involved in restoring late eighteenth- and early nineteenth-century buildings.

Firegrates are often misunderstood; from the later eighteenth century an immense variety of designs was produced. Late eighteenth-century designs with slight variations were reproduced in the late nineteenth century! The history of the firegrate is traced from the 1750s to 1939, with many examples and a growing library of catalogues.

Post Office Wall Posting-Boxes have a light-hearted appeal. However, they often appear built into Listed buildings and in Conservation Areas, and many designs were produced between 1857 and 1939. Some rare boxes are now Listed, and this study emphasises their importance to the environment.

In 1987, Charles Brooking was a joint winner of the National Art-Collections Fund prize, for his contribution to conservation. He is often consulted by public bodies as well as individuals, including the Property Services Agency, in their Richmond Terrace, Whitehall, restoration, over the sash window glazing-bar profile.

THE FUTURE OF THE COLLECTION

It is hoped that part of the Collection will form a teaching resource for students involved in architecture and the built environment, at Thames Polytechnic. This will form the basis of a major study collection in London, housed initially at Wapping. It is hoped to launch a fund-raising appeal to establish alongside this a major study centre for the use of architects, historians, and others involved in building restoration, with an emphasis on the Georgian and Victorian periods. This will encourage accurate restoration work and prevent serious mistakes. Museums such as the V & A have expressed interest in the Collection: no other such collection exists, and there is a clear need for such a resource.

A Trust was created in 1985, and the Trustees are: Colin Amery, Dan Cruickshank The Hon. William McAlpine, Colin Sorensen, Gavin Stamp, Andrew Wadsworth and A. C. Brooking. The address for the Brooking Collection is: The Brooking Collection, Woodhay, White Lane, Guildford, Surrey GU4 3PU.